Victor Paul Wierwille
and The Way International

Victor Paul Wierwille
and The Way International

J. L. Williams

MOODY PRESS

CHICAGO

ISBN: 0-8024-9233-9

Contents

Acknowledgments

I have found that writing a book is somewhat like birth—it takes a number of people to make it happen. The parents, family members, doctors, and nurses all play a crucial part. So it is with this book. It is far more than the product of one person. There are many people who have played a part in its "birth."

First, there are the many people around the country whom God used for the past several years to prod me into cultic studies. More and more, after our meetings people were coming up to me and asking, "J.L., what do you know about this group, or that group? Is it cultic, or what? Is the leader of that group correct in his theology, or is he off base?" Then there were the many heartbroken parents of young people who had become involved and were searching for answers—they had so many questions.

When confronted by such questions, I had to answer like most ministers: "I'm not really sure; I haven't researched them." Gradually, in all the questions I began to sense the Holy Spirit nudging me into doing my homework in this area. Because my master's degree work had had an emphasis on comparative world religions, I had a natural academic springboard into contemporary cultic study. So I dug into the research. Not only did I look into books and newspaper and magazine articles, but I also delved into as many personal encounters as possible with those involved with various cults and their leaders. I also began to establish communication with the few other people around the country that I knew were also involved in cultic research and exposure.

First among the other researchers was Dr. Walter Martin, foremost cult authority in America. I am indebted to him for his challenging example in this area. Also, I am very grateful for his taking the time on several occasions to discuss with me matters concerning Way doctrine. Every Christian should have his books. His *Kingdom of the Cults* is a must for every Christian's library.

Also, I am thankful to John Weldon, who told me about his research on The Way. Interaction with the brethren from Spiritual Counterfeits Project has also been invaluable. Then there are other members of the Body of Christ who are involved in researching and exposing the cults. (I have listed all the major research organizations that I am aware of in the back of this book.) There has been academic "cross-pollination" among most of us in our cultic research. I also appreciate the studies done on The Way by a fellow local minister, Pastor Gene Lepard.

One of our alumni here at the New Directions Evangelistic Association, Miss Joy Shores, has also been very helpful. Because several of her close friends became involved in cults, she has become a student of the contemporary cults and a crusader against them. The help of Joy and her mother and father, Violet and Herb, has been invaluable.

Another of our alumni, Pastor Scott Smith, helped me tremendously, especially in an analysis of the use of Greek and other biblical languages by The Way. I am indebted to his keen scholarship.

I also very much appreciate the many people around

the country who sent me newspaper articles, interviews, and papers on The Way after having read the first edition of this book. I am particularly indebted to Art Toalston for allowing me to use the tape and transcription of his interview with Victor Paul Wierwille. It has been most helpful, as you will see later in the book.

Mike Hawkins, another of our alumni, helped distribute my materials on cults in bookstores. He was also the connecting link between Moody Press and myself.

Then there are my secretaries and typists. They, as much as anyone, deserve the credit for this book. For their patient typing, retyping, and proofreading of this manuscript I am very grateful. So to Nancy Golloway, Sonia Leath, Maxine Hatley, and Joyce Salyer go my deepest thanks. You truly have the gift of helps.

To the other members of my staff who covered some of my areas of responsibility and ministry so that I could do this research and writing, I say thanks. To Joel Leath, Paul Smith, Barry Fincher, David Morrow, and especially Dick Orcutt, I am indebted.

Finally, this book is dedicated to my wife, Patt, and our four wonderful children: Trish, April, Joseph, and Jonathan. They all "loaned" their husband and father to this project. In doing so they lovingly gave up countless hours with me that were rightfully theirs.

Therefore, it is my earnest prayer that this book will help alert parents to the absolute necessity of spending *much* time with their children or young people. That is the *only* way they can establish strong emotional bonds and honest communication with them. One of the greatest needs in our country is for parents to fulfill the biblical command to teach God's Word to their children diligently (Deuteronomy 6:7) and thereby "bring them up in the discipline and instruction of the Lord" (Ephesians 6:4). If they are careful to do so, it is unlikely that their children will ever be either emotionally or spiritually vulnerable to the ever increasing number of counterfeit faiths. In the final analysis, that is the *only* solution to the cult problem.

To all the above people I say a very sincere "Thanks" and "God bless you" for all your help and prayers. You are truly partners with me in spreading the gospel (Philippians 1:5). Therefore, whatever spiritual fruit results from this book "increases to your account" (Philippians 4:17).

"Contend earnestly for the faith" (Jude 3).

1

Losing Your Way: An Introduction

Are you a prime candidate for some cults? You probably think not. But there are thousands of people just like you who also thought that about themselves. Now they are deep into one bizarre religious movement or another.

All kinds of people are vulnerable. But you say to yourself: *That could never happen to me. I would never do all of those weird things those people do—like chant, dance, eat strange foods, and sell flowers in airports and shopping centers!* And you emphatically add: *I could never be brainwashed into following some egomaniac like Jim Jones in mass suicide!*

You are thinking of only one kind of cult. Your stereotype is based either on one of those Eastern imports that is really foreign looking and acting to us Americans or on one that is led by an obvious charlatan. But what about the more subtle cults? What about the ones that really look "Christian" from all surface appearances, the ones that teach their followers about the Bible and how to witness and about being good citizens and family members? There are many of those around, and they are increasing in appeal and influence every day.

Even though that kind of cult may not lead you to do what Jim Jones led his followers to do, *spiritually and emotionally they are just as deadly*! You must remember that Jones looked very good for a long time as a preacher who really loved people. You may be a prime candidate for one of those groups.

If you have some of the following symptoms, you *are* vulnerable:

- Disillusionment and disenchantment with the institutional church

- Restlessness and discontentment with your own spiritual life

- A poor knowledge of the Bible

- Some recent disappointment or setback in your life

- A broken social relationship—separation or divorce

- An emptiness and lack of purpose and direction in your life

If you have any of the symptoms listed above, then please believe me: you are vulnerable to the cults, especially to one like The Way. Let me quote for you a letter that I received from a young woman in St. Louis, Missouri. Many of you will be able to empathize with parts or all of her story. Her name has been changed here to preserve her anonymity.

Dear Mr. Williams,

I have been a Christian for almost five years and I thought I was pretty grounded in the Word until recently. I met a guy from The Way who impressed me a great deal with his zeal for the Lord and also his knowledge of the Bible. My church recently had a big split and was severely damaged and divided because the pastor was 'found out to have enormous power and had fallen in sin. Since then,

I have been to different churches with no real sense of belonging.

This guy from the Way was very appealing and their fellowships had much to offer in meeting a lot of my needs. He came at just the right time.

I went to several meetings and attended a free introductory night for their ''Power for Abundant Living'' seminar. I was warned by other Christians about their not believing in the deity of Christ, but because they believed He is the Son of God, it seemed close enough. I was very confused and after listening to him, I didn't know if it was just tradition I clung to about the Trinity, or if they knew more about God and His Word than I did.

I believe the guy I know who is involved in The Way might be a born-again Christian, and I also know two others who definitely are (because they used to go to our church) who belong to The Way.

The battle is not over for me yet. There is a real pull to go with this guy. I have grown to really like him as a person, and it is hard for me to ignore him. Even though I know in my *mind* that Jesus is God, there is something inside me wanting to ignore it or compromise. The idea of their close fellowships and meetings all the time really appeals to me.

I don't feel like I fit into the Body of Christ. I am very scared about this whole thing and very concerned about Ron—the guy I know in The Way—and his salvation. He has been in the Way Corps and is from California and has been sent here for three years. He seems so positive and assured, and his love for the Lord seems really genuine. He reads all the commentaries written against The Way and keeps them in his files.

I never thought anything like this would ever

happen to me. I'm sorry I wrote such a long letter, but you're one person I felt would understand. Would you pray for me and also for Ron, who has a ministry in The Way. I've really grown to love him.

Thank you for your patience!

In Him,

Sue

Her story is typical. It is for sisters like Sue that I have written this book.

PURPOSE OF THE BOOK

This book is designed to answer several questions. First, are the teachings of Victor Paul Wierwille, founder of The Way, biblical? Or do they constitute "another gospel" of the sort the Bible itself condemns when it says:

> But even though we, or an angel from heaven, should preach to you a gospel contrary to that which we have preached to you, let him be accursed [Galatians 1:8].

Second, is The Way a cultic movement, or can it truly align itself with historic Christianity? Can it consider itself a part of the Body of Christ or a legitimate parachurch organization along the lines of ministries like Campus Crusade for Christ, Inter-varsity Christian Fellowship, The Navigators, and Young Life?

It is not perfectly clear at first glance by the uninitiated observer whether The Way is a cultic or Christian organization. The problem is that their members profess a belief in God and Jesus Christ, and they talk about the Holy Spirit. They accept the Bible as literally inspired by God, and so forth. Wierwille and Way people call it "the greatest loving ministry in the world!" That is a big claim. But they do act and sound loving. Their language is heavily salted with what appears to be Christian terminology: "Praise God," "Praise the Lord," "Born again," "Baptism of the Holy Spirit," "Christ our Mediator," "Christ the Son of God," "Eternal life," and other assorted familiar phrases. The Way, then, really looks and sounds good and appears very orthodox on the surface. However, when one begins to dig beneath the surface of phraseology to the bedrock of definition and meaning, a new face emerges that is far from orthodox Christianity.

It is, therefore, the open contention of this book that The Way is a cultic movement and that Victor Paul Wierwille is a false prophet in every biblical sense of the word.

The apostle Paul said, "Do not participate in the unfruitful deeds of darkness, but instead even expose them" (Ephesians 5:11). When Paul was writing to defend his apostleship against the claims of the false apostles who were invading the church at Corinth, he said:

> And what I do I will continue to do, in order to undermine the claim of those who would like to claim that in their boasted mission they work on the same terms as we do. For such men are false apostles, deceitful workmen, disguising themselves as apostles of Christ [2 Corinthians 11:12-13, RSV].*

That is exactly what Victor Paul Wierwille does; for he claims that he has purified Christianity of its perversions and got it back to its first-century base. So, because of his claims and the rapid growth of the movement, I personally feel the compulsion of Jude when he said: "I felt the necessity to write to you appealing that you contend earnestly for the faith which was once for all delivered to the saints" (Jude 3).

There is one thing I would like to make clear at the

---

*Revised Standard Version.

beginning of this study. This book is not meant in *any way* to slander Mr. Wierwille or his followers personally. I believe that for the most part they are sincere and dedicated people, even though from a biblical standpoint they are *sincerely wrong*. Therefore, they are misguided in their dedication and zeal. In relation to this they are very similar to the Jews of Paul's day, whom the apostle described as follows: "I can testify about them that they are zealous for God, but their zeal is not based on knowledge" (Romans 10:2, NIV).†

So, even though I intend to be as firm and as destructive as I can possibly be to Mr. Wierwille's false doctrine, I mean no personal slander against him. I am commanded to love him as a person for whom Christ died. I do love him, although I totally reject with my whole being his heretical and apostate teachings. I join with other Christians in praying for his salvation. What a victory it would be for the Kingdom of God if he would repent, reject his false teachings, and come into the Body of Christ. His talents and gifts could then be used positively for the edification rather than the destruction of the Body of Christ.

The purposes of this book, then, are several:

- To expose The Way for the cultic organization that it is;

- To cause those who are already involved in it to reevaluate the movement in the light of God's Word;

- To deter others who might be vulnerable to this and other such cults because of inadequate scriptural knowledge; and

- To strengthen other brothers and sisters in the faith with a sound apologetic (defense) for the deity of Christ and the triunity of God.

---

† *The New International Version.*

2

The Doctor:
Victor Paul Wierwille

To understand The Way you must understand its founder, Victor Paul Wierwille. He is alternately described as loving, warm, and compassionate, and as hot-tempered, power-hungry, and autocratic. The description you get just depends upon whom you talk to. As a public speaker, he has a charisma that is coupled with a keen flair for show business. He is an astute organizer and motivator. In 1976, Dunn and Bradstreet's financial report said that Wierwille is a "showman, promoter and excellent businessman." In conversation he can be very persuasive; but when contradicted he can quickly become caustic, defensive, and bombastic. Many interviewers have temporarily enjoyed his charm, only to see it turn quickly into sarcastic raving when they dared to question or criticize him.

To all his loyal followers, Wierwille is affectionately known as "The Doctor." This promotes respect and supports his reputation as a Bible scholar and teacher. He is both founder and president of The Way International. Obviously, that has not always been his position.

WIERWILLE'S HISTORY: THE MAKING OF A HERETIC

Victor Paul Wierwille was born on December 31, 1916, in the kitchen of the family farmhouse. Life for him started on the 147-acre, Shelby County, Ohio, farm that is now the international headquarters of The Way movement. He was the youngest of seven children. He grew up in the fundamental atmosphere of the Evangelical and Reformed Church, now known as the United Church of Christ. It seems that from his youth he wanted to be a minister. He says that when he was eight or nine he met a speaker who had come to his home church. The minister asked Wierwille what he wanted to be when he grew up. "A man of God like you," he responded.[1] His brother recalls that Wierwille used to practice by preaching to the trees in the woods on the family farm.

Wierwille attended a one-room schoolhouse until the sixth grade. He then attended the New Knoxville School, where he was an average student. A conflict with the superintendent resulted in his expulsion from school. But he returned, determined to achieve. He worked hard, he says, and developed into a good student.[2] In 1934 he graduated from the New Knoxville High School. Basketball was his love and he excelled in it—so much so that he was offered a scholarship by Ohio State University. His father said no to that offer, however, because he wanted him to go to Mission House College.

Even as a young person, Wierwille's abilities to influence people were known. Vince McKelvey, a staff writer for the Dayton (Ohio) *Journal Herald,* quotes a local resident who went to school with Wierwille:

> "If anybody had a $5 bill, he had it. . . . He has always been an outgoing guy, wanting to be popular."
>
> He was "always figuring" some way of being the one who knew something special, the man said, adding Wierwille wanted to be the center of attention, "that's for sure."[3]

Three years after he graduated from high school, Wierwille secretly married his high-school sweetheart,

Dorothea Kipp, or Dotsie, as he affectionately calls her. That was in 1937, and she had just graduated from nurses' training. He then went to Mission House College, where he, like many college students, struggled with his vocation. He first considered medicine, then law, but finally decided on the ministry.

From Mission House, he went to Princeton Theological Seminary in 1940, and speaks highly of his professors there.[4] He also took some correspondence courses on the Bible from Moody Bible Institute and even taught homiletics (preaching) briefly at Gordon Divinity School.

In 1941, he was ordained a minister in the denomination in which he was raised. His first pastorate was in Payne, Ohio. That ministry lasted three years. Wierwille recalls that he served earnestly while he was there.[5] In 1944, he received a call from a church in Van Wert, Ohio, that had an active membership of approximately twenty-one. He accepted the call.

Wierwille's success as a local pastor was mixed. He thinks that his ministry through the Van Wert church was at best only moderately successful. Frustration would probably be a better word to describe his feelings. He just could not seem to produce the changed behavior that Christians are supposed to manifest. He reflected back on those early days this way:

> As I looked about me at the communities where I had worked, the abundant life was frequently not evident. In contrast to these Christian people, I could see that the secular world of non-Christians was manifesting a more abundant life than were the members of the church.[6]

The Missionary Who Changed His Life

As he continued to struggle with the lack of power in his own life and ministry, Wierwille met a missionary who had just returned from China. Her name was Rosalind Rinker. His encounter with her ultimately changed both the course and the emphasis of his entire ministry. Wierwille heard her speak and was so impressed that he invited her to visit him in Payne. She came late in the summer of 1942. During that visit, Miss Rinker urged Wierwille to align his life with the Bible. She greatly impressed Wierwille with her belief in the Bible as the Word of God. He says he had never heard that in all his years of schooling—or in any case had not believed.

The last night of her stay with Wierwille was a turning point for him. As Miss Rinker and Wierwille knelt in the church, he prayed, asking for forgiveness, love, and understanding. He recalls telling God that if He desired his service, then He would have to work, for Wierwille himself felt despairing.[7]

How about their relationship today? "She won't have much to do with me now—because our positions on the Holy Spirit differ," he says.[8] A little later we shall see why neither Miss Rinker nor any others in orthodox Christianity agree with his doctrine of the Holy Spirit. But Wierwille still acknowledges her as the one who was instrumental in his return to the Bible, with which he had been brought up, and whose principles he had forgotten during his seminary days.[9] Unfortunately, Wierwille's seminary experience did to him what it has done to scores of other ministers; it undermined his belief in the Bible as the Word of God. Most of the men Wierwille studied under were either liberal or neo-orthodox. To some degree they must bear the responsibility for the direction of Wierwille's life and ministry.

THE AUDIBLE VOICE OF GOD

After Miss Rinker left, Wierwille continued his search. It was while he was sitting in his office one day that the real turning point came. He says that is when God spoke to him audibly:

> I was praying. And I told Father outright that He could have the whole thing, unless there were real genuine answers that I wouldn't ever have to back up on.

> And that's when He spoke to me audibly, just like I'm talking to you now. He said He would teach me the Word as it had not been known since the first century if I would teach it to others.

> Well, I nearly flew off my chair. I couldn't believe that God would talk to me. . . . But He spoke to me just as plainly as I'm talking now to you.[10]

Wierwille quickly began to wonder and doubt about this audible communication from God. The next day he prayed that he might be given a sign to assure him that God had in fact spoken to him. He says that God gave him that sign:

> The sky was crystal blue and clear. Not a cloud in sight. It was a beautiful early autumn day. I said, "If that was really you, and you meant what you said, give me a sign. Let me see it snow." My eyes were tightly shut as I prayed. And then I opened them.

> The sky was so white and thick with snow, I couldn't see the tanks at the filling station on the corner not 75 feet away.[11]

When questioned about this encounter and God's audible conversation with him, Wierwille emphatically said:

> Man, if God isn't talking to people today, you better get on talkin' terms with God. Why shouldn't He speak to us? You see, it seems like you're a freak if God talks to you. Maybe the freaks are on the other side if He doesn't talk to you! . . . If my father didn't talk to me, I'd get me a new father. If He can't talk to me, but my earthly father can, then

my heavenly Father is less than my earthly father, and that, to me, is almost blasphemy.[12]

Most Christians would have little problem with the fact of God speaking to us. We communicate with Him regularly. It is the audible part that bothers us. We do not say that God cannot speak to us that way, but it certainly is not His normal means of communicating with man. A reporter further quizzed Wierwille on this matter and said that he was a Christian who communicated with God regularly—but not audibly. Wierwille replied: "If you did [hear God speak audibly to you] you might fall over dead, 'cause you're not expectin' it either. . . . You haven't acclimatized to listen to God."[13]

PRELUDES TO THE WAY

One of Wierwille's earlier attempts to reach out to the world of young people was a radio program begun on October 2, 1942, on station WLOK (now WIMA) in Lima, Ohio. It was called the "Chimes Hour Youth Caravan" and was incorporated in 1947 "for the furtherance of the gospel of Jesus Christ by radio and personal appearances."

Wierwille stated later that that broadcast and his Sunday morning service impelled him to go to the Word of God for new teachings each week.[14]

Wierwille continued to try to find the key to change man's behavior spiritually. He began to concentrate on the words of Christ recorded in John 10:10: "I came that they might have life, and might have it abundantly." He became increasingly convinced that that verse was the key to spiritual success. So he began to erect a theological program around it. Gradually that gave birth in 1953 to what he called "Power for Abundant Living." Over the years that course grew, further evolved, and gradually became what it is today. Now, the PFAL, as it is referred to in abbreviation, is the cornerstone of The Way movement. More will be said about it later.

The Break from the Church

In 1955 the corporation name was changed to The Way, Incorporated, and the ministry purposes were expanded to include "television, the printed page (and) licensing ministers . . . to send forth qualified men and women to foreign fields, (to) promote biblical education."[15] Two years later, frustrated about the church and growing more excited about his new movement, Wierwille resigned his Van Wert, Ohio, United Church of Christ pulpit to give himself full-time to The Way. He had gone to Van Wert to minister to a congregation of twenty-one. By the time he left the church in 1957, the sanctuary was regularly filled for Sunday services.[16]

Looking back at his years in Van Wert, Wierwille sees them as formative. He says it was there that he began his search in earnest, and during that period the Bible became exciting to him.[17] The search of those years caused Wierwille to become disappointed and disillusioned with most of the books he had read. He says he took several hundred volumes of his library out to the city dump and disposed of them.

During his Van Wert years he also came under the influence of people like Rufus Moseley and the healing ministry of Glenn Clark. He became a theological eclectic, picking and choosing from many sources. A patchwork theology began to develop. Increasingly, his thoughts and theology conflicted with his denomination's beliefs. A parting of the ways seemed inevitable, and finally Wierwille resigned. According to church records, the resignation was not entirely voluntary. It seems that some problems had arisen on a mission tour to India, where Wierwille had gone to visit some of the work of his denomination. On that tour he made critical remarks about both his church and the Indian government. A 1976 letter by Harvey Zuern, former northwest Ohio synod president of the United Church of Christ, said:

> Because of certain remarks which (Wierwille) made criticizing the Church and the Government of India, a riot erupted in one of our stations.
>
> Upon his return to Ohio, a (church) committee . . . conducted a hearing with Mr. Wierwille. Because of his feelings and attitudes for the church, he was advised to withdraw as a minister.[18]

BACK TO THE FARM

Several years after he resigned his pulpit, Wierwille moved The Way from Van Wert to his family's Shelby County farm near New Knoxville, Ohio. The Way was financed in large part in those days by Wierwille's older brother Harry, who had done well in the upholstery business. The family farm is still the nerve center and international headquarters of The Way. But Wierwille's success was still only moderate in those days. David Anderson, who was The Way's first outreach director but who left it in 1973, said of those early years, "We prayed for years, 'Lord just send us the people.' " Anderson also quoted Wierwille as saying, "There's a tremendous amount of truth here that we have in this word of God and I can teach it . . . But I don't know how to get the people."[19] It was Anderson who came up with the suggestion to film the PFAL course and then tour the country with it. In 1963 Wierwille had made his first attempt at using film. He did a black and white videotaped television program in Lima, Ohio, called "The Teacher." When Anderson saw some of those programs, he got the idea to put the PFAL on film. That first filming of the course cost them thirty thousand dollars. The idea worked, and the timing seemed right.

THE RIGHT OPPORTUNITY

It was 1968, and the Jesus Movement was growing.

Suddenly Wierwille had a market of countercultural
young people who were not attracted to traditional
churches but who were still seeking spiritual reality.
Many were disillusioned, empty, and "burned out."
They had no cause, no purpose to give themselves to.
Many turned from drugs, sex, and activism to religion.
Some of those young people found true spiritual reality
in Jesus Christ and gradually became a part of some
Christian body. Many more did not. Many of them were
picked off by the Children of God, Hare Krishna, and
Sun Myung Moon, among others. Wierwille also got his
share. In 1967 and 1968, Wierwille made several trips to
California. He visited and ministered in the Haight-
Ashbury district of San Francisco. He began to pick up a
few followers, and he invited them to New Knoxville for
the summer. The next year more came. That opened the
floodgate. Wierwille's personal secretary, Rhoda Wierwille (she married Wierwille's brother Reuben), recalls
that young people, most of them long-haired hippies,
began coming to New Knoxville after Wierwille's
California trip. She says his ministry "made things fit for
them."[20]

I believe those young people became vulnerable to The
Way and other contemporary cults for several reasons.
Many of them had already lost interest in the institutional
church. They would no longer look in that direction for
help. Others who had not had a church heritage went to
the various movements to find a spiritual home. Some of
them first tried the church, but because they were not
"straight" they were often rejected. Many in the organized church were not ready for their faded jeans,
T-shirts, long hair, beards, bare feet, guitars, and spon-
taneity. Those young people then became prime candi-
dates for the various cultic groups who were offering
religion—but without the rigid institutionalism that the
young people had previously known. Most of them were

also biblically unprepared to recognize and handle theological error. Besides, they were finding in the cults the emotional gratification they were looking for; that is what people are usually seeking in religion. The theological issues always play a secondary role to the emotional reinforcement. It is still true that *until love is felt, the message is not heard*. So, because many of the cultic groups were talking about and expressing love, they were rapidly gaining loyal followers. That is when The Way began to grow. Their people breakthrough had come.

Thus the real beginning of The Way is difficult to pinpoint. A 1977 Way magazine pictures Wierwille with the headline "Celebrating Thirty-Five Years of Biblical Research and Teaching." That would put its origin back in the early 1940s. As we have already seen, that is unrealistic because he did not resign his Van Wert, Ohio, pulpit until 1957. Even though The Way was incorporated three years earlier, its real beginning numerically was not until the start of the Jesus Movement in 1968. That is the date that I would suggest for its real beginning.

WIERWILLE THE DOCTOR

That is a little about Wierwille and the early days of The Way. Now let us look briefly at his qualifications as a "Doctor," Bible scholar, and teacher. We have already looked at most of his educational background, except for the matter of his doctorate. His latest book gives his total academic pedigree as follows: He received a Bachelor of Divinity degree from Mission House (Lakeland) College and Seminary. He was a student at the University of Chicago, and then earned a Master of Theology degree from Princeton Theological Seminary. Later he received his doctorate from an unnamed institution.[21]

Wierwille in fact received his doctorate from Pike's Peak Bible Seminary, which is reputed to be a "degree mill.'' That assessment is probably an overstatement. However, a letter from an official of the Colorado Commission on Higher Education says, ''Pikes Peak Seminary had no resident instruction, no published list of faculty, no accreditation, and no agency of the government supervised it. It offered its degree programs by 'extramural' methods, involving the sending of book reviews and papers by mail.''[22] Otto G. Ruff, who resigned in 1978 after nineteen years as Colorado's director of teacher certification and accreditation, said that Pike's Peak was a nonaccredited correspondence school and that its degrees were not recognized by any other institution. Ruff further said that Pike's Peak did not fit the pattern of ''degree mills'' because there was some work required. But the requirements were minimal when compared with major universities.''[23] But if it is not a ''degree mill,'' Pike's Peak * is certainly not a widely recognized graduate school of biblical studies, either. Wierwille admits that many seminaries recognize neither Pike's Peak Seminary nor his doctor's degree.[24] However, he contended in an interview with Art Toalston of the *National Courier,* ''If you wanna give me a PhD exam in my field, I'm willing to take it.''[25] I do not want to dwell too much on the school from which he got his doctor's degree. But inasmuch as Way members do so by always referring to him as ''the Doctor''—and almost reverencing him as the greatest Bible scholar and teacher of the day—I think it needs to be emphasized that Pike's Peak does not have the reputation of producing great Bible scholars. Also, it may be that no deception is intended by omission of the school from the list of institutions at which he received his formal education, but

---

*''Pike's Peak changed its name several times after it's incorporation in 1927. Following the death of its president, Fred E. Stemme, in 1965, it became Colorado Bible College and Seminary. In 1969, it was moved to Chicago under a new name, Evangelical Bible College and Seminary'' (*Christianity Today,* November 21, 1975, pp. 19-20).

Pike's Peak is rather conspicuous by its absence.

WIERWILLE'S THEOLOGY

What is Wierwille's theology? As we have seen, it is a cut-and-paste patchwork. Wierwille's theology is a blend of Unitarianism, dispensationalism, Calvinism, and Pentecostalism—a strange theological mixture. He defines an apostle as "one who brings new light to his generation." Because he himself claims to have received audible communication from God, presumably he fills that role. He is apparently viewed as such by many of his followers. Elena Whiteside writes of one Way member who views Dr. Wierwille as the next man of God to appear on the scene after the death of Paul.[26] Way books and magazines are filled with statements of praise and adoration—almost worship—of Wierwille. His presence, they say, arouses excitement and anticipation.[27]

His followers shower him with love and affection, and he returns it. He constantly says to them:

> You're my kids. . . . You're beautiful. . . . You're just the greatest! . . . You're God's best! . . . The greatest young people in the world came up out of the Way Ministry! The finest students in America today are Way students! You are the most beautiful men and women of God the world has ever seen. Let them see you—they haven't seen any in centuries![28]

It is clear, then, that Wierwille and his followers believe him to be a prophet of God. In one of his books he says that he must be listened to and obeyed as Paul was. After urging his readers to obey his instructions down to the finest detail, Wierwille quotes the words of Paul in 1 Thessalonians 2:13: "When ye received the word of God which ye heard of us, ye received it not as the word of men, but as it is in truth, the word of God." Wierwille then says:

If you will be as honest with God as that Word of God says, you too can walk into the greatness of the manifestation of the power of God. But if you think this is just Victor Paul Wierwille writing or speaking to you, you will never receive. If you know that what I am saying to you are words which the Holy Ghost has spoken and is speaking to you through my ministry and my life, then you too will manifest forth the greatness of the power of God.[29]

SUMMARY

There can be little doubt that Wierwille believes in what he is saying. No doubt he believes he is God's man of the hour. This study and recounting of his spiritual pilgrimage has been a saddening experience for me as I consider his talents; his sincere searching; his disillusioning seminary education that eroded his belief in the authority and integrity of the Bible; his quest for reality; his contact with so many good spiritual people; his energy, creativity, and zeal; his "vision"; his audible encounter with "God"; his separation from the Body of Christ; his jettisoning of church history; and his heresy.

Wierwille probably did have some kind of encounter with or visitation from the spirit world. However, because of the nature of the "revelation" he received, and because it stands contrary to both Scripture and Christian history, I believe that his visitation was from "Satan [who] disguises himself as an angel of light" (2 Corinthians 11:14). The apostle Paul's stern warning to the Christians at Galatia is still God's word to us today concerning those kinds of revelations: "But even though we, or an angel from heaven, should preach to you a gospel contrary to that which we have preached to you, let him be accursed" (Galatians 1:8).

What a serious warning his life is to every believer!

"No prophecy of Scripture is a matter of one's own interpretation" (2 Peter 1:20, emphasis added). His story reminds us that you can come from a good family and have the right church background, a good education, and countless contacts with good, spiritual people. You can have talent, vision, creativity, and zeal. But cut off from the correctives and checks and balances of the Body of Christ, you can still end up in spiritual individualism and theological heresy. And in it all, you can be very sincere—but sincerely wrong. In your desire to serve God, you can easily become unwittingly duped into being an ally of the archenemy of the Kingdom, all the while believing that you are serving God. In the process, you can lose not only your own soul, but, like Wierwille, you can lead hundreds—even thousands— down that same road to destruction. Both Wierwille and members of The Way sincerely believe that they are right. But the Bible's warning still sounds forth: "There is a way which seems right to a man, but its end is the way of death" (Proverbs 14:12).

What fantastic potential Victor Paul Wierwille has for the Kingdom of God. Every Christian needs to start praying that he might humble himself, repent of his errors, and return to the faith that he was raised in as a boy. Until such time, however, I must in Christian love continue to "contend earnestly for the faith which was once for all delivered to the saints" (Jude 3) and stand against Wierwille's heresy. Toward both him and The Way I must continue to take the stand that Paul took against the false prophets of his day who were setting themselves up as true apostles of God: "And I will keep on doing what I am doing in order to cut the ground from under those who want an opportunity to be considered equal with us in the things they boast about" (2 Corinthians 11:12, NIV).

3

The Tree:
The Way Organization

In 1973, The Way's income was reported to be $20,000. By 1978 its assets were listed at $9.7 million. Wierwille also has at his disposal a twin-engine turbojet that seats about twenty people, two deluxe motor coaches for national tours, a college,* publishing facilities, a computer center, a bookstore, an historical

---

*The Way purchased what was previously a United Presbyterian college in Emporia, Kansas. The school had been forced to close in 1973 because of financial problems. The Way paid off a mortgage of $504,000 plus debts of $190,000, including 1973 salaries of the defunct school's former teachers. Total renovations of the school are estimated by Wierwille to be $2.5 million. The 41-acre campus has now become "The Way College." It opened in the fall of 1974 with a student body of over 400. Wierwille has referred to the transaction as a switch in affiliation rather than a purchase, thereby hoping to retain the accreditation granted the Presbyterian school, which was founded in 1892. Thus far that hope has not been realized, and the school has neither accreditation nor the authority to confer degrees. Their college catalogue states this in its purpose: "We will remain absolutely nonsectarian as a Christian school teaching the self-interpreted accuracy of the Word of God and not any person or group's opinion about it" (p. 3).

center, an outreach service center, several camps—and the organization is still growing. All of this is controlled by a three-member board of directors, with Wierwille as president.

Whatever his theological errors, Wierwille is definitely an able and astute organizer. He has organized the entire Way organization around the structure of a tree: The *roots* are the international headquarters at New Knoxville, the *trunk* is the regions into which the nation is divided, the *limbs* are state headquarters, the *branches* are the various cities, the *twigs* are the home or campus meetings, and the *leaves* are the individual followers. The leaf is where the fruit is. The organization's brochure *This Is the Way* describes the twig fellowships as follows:

> Like a tree, the "life" of the ministry is in the twig (where the leaves cluster), where the accuracy of God's Word is taught oftentimes daily, as during the First Century Church. It is here in the twig that each believer becomes "rooted and grounded and established" in his knowledge and practical application of the Word.

College twig fellowships are strategic for The Way. That is why they usually have their headquarters near campuses. The brochure describes the college twig ministry as an arm of the Department of College and Correctional Outreach. Twig groups meet daily on numbers of campuses, and WOW (Word Over the World) leaders conduct Power for Abundant Living classes.

The Way organization is thus fashioned after a tree. The big question though is whether The Way tree is in reality the "tree of life" or the "tree of error." Is its fruit theologically good or poisonous? We shall see when we analyze The Way's theology in a later section.

How Big Is the Tree?

It is difficult to determine accurately how many followers The Way has. There are no official Way members, a point they constantly emphasize. They do not have members—only "believers." Most estimates, however, are in the twenty-to-thirty thousand range. Some would say more, some would say less. At its national headquarters, The Way currently employs about three hundred full- and part-time staff members who are seeking to run and expand the Way ministry.

Wierwille's followers are now reportedly distributed in all fifty states and in fifty foreign countries. The movement is appealing to many and growing because it criticizes the established nominal churches and their lack of power and conviction. Even though they say that they do not criticize the established church, Way members do so very often. A Way member from Rye, New York, declared that denominations are made by men and that the fellowship of Way members at New Knoxville is nearer the first-century church than anything else in today's world.[1] Anyone who has ever attended a Way meeting or heard Wierwille speak will testify to his constant attacks upon the church. He says denominations are interested in self-perpetuation rather than in teaching the Bible,[2] and that "so-called Christianity is going down the drain, losing, has lost and will continue to lose."[3] Yet Wierwille is quick to drop the names of nationally and internationally known theologians or religious leaders that he has supposedly studied with to lend credence to himself and his movement. Consider the following statement found in most biographies about Wierwille:

> Dr. Wierwille visited E. Stanley Jones and studied his Ashram program. Such men as Glenn Clark, Rufus Moseley, Starr Daily, Albert Cliffe, Bishop K. C. Pillai and others were guests of Dr. Wierwil-

le's local congregation. Karl Barth of Switzerland was a friend and consultant, as well as other European and Far Eastern scholars. With these men Dr. Wierwille quested for biblical enlightenment.[4]

I cannot speak for all the above mentioned men and their relationships with Wierwille, but I do know about the late E. Stanley Jones. Wierwille may have studied Jones's Ashram movement, but he certainly did not study or adopt any of Jones's theology. The late missionary to India and the world was solidly evangelical and biblically orthodox. He would thoroughly repudiate Wierwille's doctrine if he were alive and knew that his name was being associated with such a heresy. One of my seminary professors and friends, Dr. J. T. Seamands, is one of the seven people who now guide the Ashram movement. He has repudiated, on behalf of E. Stanley Jones and the Ashram movement, any support of or agreement with Wierwille's doctrine or movement. So Wierwille is unquestionably guilty of false association and "name dropping" in his effort to gain support for and lend credence to his movement.

Not only do those in The Way say that they do not have members, but they also say that they are not a church. According to Way publicity folders, The Way "is not a church, nor is it a denomination or a religious sect of any sort." However, it has ordained over fifty clergymen, some of whom are women, and all of them are authorized to perform marriages, lead in worship, serve Communion, and so on. And if a person becomes a member of The Way, he usually soon ceases all participation in and support of his previous church. So in spite of the amount of verbal camouflage its adherents use or the constant statements they make to the contrary, The Way is in reality a *church substitute* for its followers—one, in fact, that promises its followers power, certainty, the overcoming of all fears and failures, and even deliverance from physical illness.

The Way emphasizes daily meetings in homes, breaking of bread (the Lord's Supper), tithing, and witnessing. The strong emphasis on *how* to live the abundant life, coupled with a concern for the individual; the offer of an existential encounter with God through His Holy Spirit; and a stressing of the centrality of the Scriptures all make The Way very appealing to many people— especially young people—today. The Way's promotional brochure *This Is the Way* declares that The Way International is a "biblical research and teaching" body interested in helping people know, through the truth of the Bible, God's power in their lives.

That really sounds good and has appeal. As previously stated, the people who are especially vulnerable are the ones who either have no religious faith at all or who have become disenchanted with their institutional church involvement. People from conservative church backgrounds are especially vulnerable. *This Is The Way* states that the movement's adherents are men and women of differing backgrounds whose spiritual yearnings have long been unsatisfied. It quotes Christ's promise: "I am come that ye might have life, and that ye might have it more abundantly" (John 10:10).

It all sounds very orthodox and acceptable, does it not? However, as we shall see later, it is in reality what Christ warned us of when He said: "Beware of the false prophets, who come to you in sheep's clothing, but inwardly are ravenous wolves. You will know them by their fruits" (Matthew 7:15-16*a*).

OTHER IMPORTANT WAY NAMES TO KNOW

As I pointed out earlier, the PFAL, or "Power for Abundant Living" course, is the fundamental outreach tool of The Way organization. The Way's brochure gives a glowing description of the course. Power for Abundant Living is said to deal with all the scriptural keys that make victory possible for the believer in any circumstance of life. Also promised are the fulfillment of deep-seated desires and a "life of rich abundance."

Way leaders make a big effort to get everyone to take this course. In fact, a person cannot be considered a true follower of The Way who has not taken the PFAL course. A typical "sales talk" for the PFAL course will assure the listener that the course is extremely helpful because the person taking it can as a result understand those things God wants him to know.[5]

I heard Wierwille say this at a Way rally:

> The Bible is not difficult! God wrote it so we could understand it. The reason this book is so difficult is because that's what we've been told it was! It isn't difficult. If you take our course we will give you all of the keys to God's Word so you can unlock it for yourself, so you can understand it.[6]

The PFAL is *the* initiation and confirmation course for the organization, as well as its chief source of revenue. It has become the induction and indoctrination center for the entire movement. Through it, Wierwille has his chief tool to propagate his hybrid theology. The entire course consists of fifteen taped sessions, each approximately three hours long. In those lectures, Wierwille gives his "keys to abundant living." Students are reportedly being recruited at a rate of one thousand per month, all at the going rate of $100 each for the course. The first PFAL began in August 1968 at a charge of $20. It later went up to $65, then $85, and now $100. Then there is an advanced course for $250. However, The Way emphasizes that this is not a fee or charge but a "required minimum donation." If you cannot make the donation, however, you cannot take the course.

The PFAL is advertised as a "biblical research class."

Because biblical principles are emphasized as the way to a successful life, it is not surprising that many people have their lives changed in some way by the course. As Shakespeare said: "Gold is still gold, even if it is in a fool's or thief's pocket." There is some truth taught in the course, and that is what brings any positive changes, not Wierwille's errors. Satan always seeks to hide 10 percent error in 90 percent of truth! Dr. Jack Sparks, a former professor of behavioral psychology, says this about the PFAL course and the changes brought about by it:

> Ignoring the very basic foundational doctrines of the Church, he put together a patchwork system of heretical biblical interpretation. But the system could effect certain behavioral modifications that were satisfactory for his purposes . . . he could produce some results. There are, of course, many avenues to behavior modification. Wierwille had found one of them and worked it to the full. Cloaked with a familiar-sounding evangelical vocabulary, the product had a market.[7]

With these principles gained from the PFAL, which Wierwille has "researched," one is on his or her way to "abundant living." Wierwille's emphasis is on the complete attainability of the abundant life in the here and now. The PFAL course that will supposedly give anyone "all of the basic keys" to attaining this life seems to be the very heart of the movement's success. Concerning these "how tos" of abundant living, one Ohio leader said: "We don't tell people *what* they should do, but *how* they should do it. We feel that in God's Word are the keys to abundant life—when they are told *how to*, then a bureaucracy is not needed to control them—they function and share with others about The Way."[8] Obviously, this lack of bureaucracy and rigid structure is highly welcomed by a generation already emphasizing freedom, informality, and "do-your-own-thing-ism."

But is this the abundant life that Jesus talked about? I think not. Concerning the PFAL course—as well as The Way in general—I have to agree sadly with Kevin N. Springer, who also analyzed The Way and concluded as follows: "Is this abundant life? I think not. The Way is well organized and is emphasizing certain doctrines . . . that are sucking many into their sect. Yet, in the final analysis The Way is only abundantly leading people to hell."[9]

WOW AMBASSADORS

Word Over The World (WOW) Ambassadors carry on the outreach of The Way. According to *This Is The Way,* the Ambassadors are youth who spend at least one year in a witnessing, caring, and teaching ministry. They hold part-time jobs to support themselves.

At a Way rally I attended in Raleigh, North Carolina, "Uncle Harry," Wierwille's now deceased older brother, said this about the WOW program: "Go on WOW for one year; it will be the greatest training you will ever have this side of heaven!" The WOWs are very much like the missionaries of the Mormon Church. They are self-supporting and must tithe at least 10 percent to the national headquarters. They are the ones who really get out on the grass-roots level and enlist participation in the PFAL classes.

In 1974, 1,033 WOW Ambassadors were sent out to the midwest, south, and southwest sections of the United States for one year of missionary service. More than twice that number, 2,077, were commissioned in August 1975 for duty in the eastern United States, Canada, and Germany; and 104 "Minute Men" (veteran missionaries) received western United States assignments. Their projections for WOWs are: 12,448 by 1980;

72,024 by 1983; 219,084 by 1985; and 3,220,000 by 1990 (statistics given at a Way rally in Raleigh, N.C.). You cannot say that they do not dream and plan big.

Leadership for the organization is provided through a training program (The Way Corps) that was begun in 1970. The program emphasizes discipline and sacrifice for propagation of The Way. Potential leaders are chosen to live and study with their teacher for two years.[10]

So the emphasis is always toward progressively more involvement. First one is challenged to take the PFAL. Then he is challenged to step out on faith and become a Way missionary through the WOW program for at least one year. After that the challenge is for the two-year Way Corps program, which usually leads to permanent Way leadership.

THE WAY MAGAZINE

The Way Magazine is the official periodical of The Way organization. It is subtitled: *For People Who Love God and His Word*. The magazine has increased fourfold in circulation over the past three and one-half years, to over ten thousand. It is a four-color, attractively done magazine. Each issue is filled with pictures of smiling, happy people who are supposedly finding abundant living through The Way movement. Each issue features a lead article by Wierwille, reports on various Way activities, advertisements for his various books, and a constant promotion of the PFAL courses. Aside from the theological content, the magazine would be a credit and tribute to any organization. Its technical quality is both excellent and appealing.

CORRECTIONAL OUTREACH

The Way has a prison ministry as a part of its outreach. Way leaders claim to have prison works in about one hundred institutions spread through thirty states. Under the auspices of The Way's "Department of College and Correctional Outreach, PFAL classes and twig fellowships are conducted in both federal and state prisons.[11]

They claim that 97 percent of the inmates who take their PFAL class have not returned to prison. So their correctional director has said: "The greatest and most effective means for correction begins with the class on Power for Abundant Living."[12]

I travel into prisons across the country each year in my own ministry, and in many of those prisons I have found The Way organization. The members' zeal again is commendable, but I am not convinced of the validity of charging the inmates $100 for the PFAL course. But inmates have to pay like anyone else. Most prisoners I have met could probably better spend that money on the many personal and family needs they have. Besides that, in every prison I know of there are *free* Bible study courses available. Groups like the Yokefellows, Gideons, Fellowship Foundation, Teen Challenge, and a host of others offer them. With all of those courses, both the content and the price are better than that of the PFAL course.

FAMILY CAMPS

The Way sponsors family camping for Way followers and families. I heard Wierwille speak one time when he was on his way to Boca Raton, Florida, where he was opening and dedicating a new family camp that his organization had recently purchased there. Since that time The Way has also bought and dedicated one in Colorado called "Camp Gunnison" family ranch.

POLITICAL OUTREACH

Wierwille has also established a political outreach program called T.W.I.G. (The Word in Government).

The purpose of this program is to train young people for political involvement, and it has been tested in Maine, where one of the state senators is reportedly a Way supporter. Concerning this program, Wierwille made the following statements at the Way rally I attended in Raleigh, North Carolina:

> We're going to train people how to get into the political field and work in it. There is no training in any college or university like we are going to do!

> Prepare and sooner or later they will have to elect you because you will be the best person for the job—because you are the best!

> When the day comes for you to be an ambassador, you will represent the U.S. in the most admirable way. . . . When you get to be governors and senators you will know what to do. . . . We need people to work in city and local governments and on the school boards who will put the integrity and accuracy of God's Word first!

> Our political WOWs have already helped to elect a mayor—the first woman mayor ever elected in the state of Maine—and she knows we did it—and immediately she registered for our PFAL class! Her daughter had already taken it!

> They are already schooling our political WOWs for the Republican national convention as voting delegates!

ROCK OF AGES CHRISTIAN MUSIC FESTIVAL

The Rock of Ages festival is a sort of national convention for the movement. Concluding The Way's summer program, this weekend gathering features music, Bible instruction, and joyful celebration.[13]

The first such festival was held at the farm in New Knoxville in 1971, with an attendance of 1,000. In 1974,

41

the event was held at the county fairgrounds, with 5,500 full-time registrants plus several thousand part-timers who attended evening sessions. In August 1975, they had a four-day festival at the Lima, Ohio, fairgrounds, with more than 8,300 attending (at twenty-five dollars per person). There were fifty states and a dozen foreign countries represented at that event. Each evening, "The Way Chorale Internationale," one of their musical groups that is 500 voices strong, performed gospel rock music.

THE AMERICAN CHRISTIAN PRESS

The American Christian Press is the Way's own printing firm that prints Wierwille's books, pamphlets, and *The Way Magazine*.

MONEY

About now you may be asking yourself, How is all of this financed? We have already seen that the proceeds from the PFAL classes total millions of dollars per year. Also, all Way followers must tithe a minimum of 10 percent, and the emphasis is upon giving even more. The emphasis is that "we receive from God on the basis of our giving." *Every penny of the tithes goes to the national headquarters.* Not a dime can stay in the local fellowships. They must ask the national headquarters for any money they receive.

It seems to be unknown how much Wierwille personally makes. All Way leaders will say is that it is "remarkably small." However, Wierwille does not have to make a large salary when you realize that his home is completely furnished and that he has access to The Way's resources, including cars, a plane, and deluxe motor coaches. One ex-Way staffer, David Anderson, said: "Everything I've ever known about the guy (Wierwille), he's sold out for money."[14] One thing is certain: all The

Way's financial resources are consolidated under the control of the organization's three trustees—Wierwille, his son Donald, and Howard Allen. And can anyone doubt who makes the final decisions on that board of trustees, inasmuch as Wierwille is president of the board?

SUMMARY

From the above organizational survey, you can see that The Way today is certainly no small, parochial, struggling operation. It is constantly expanding and diversifying its outreach. All the things I have mentioned above are being duplicated in most states and in many countries of the world. Again, Wierwille's organizational skill must be recognized and the zeal and dedication of Way members acknowledged. Increasingly they will be a force for the Christian faith to contend with, especially because their WOW missionaries are spreading across the world with Wierwille's gospel—which on the surface sounds and looks so much like the real thing. Their presence and influence will increasingly cause confusion among non-Christians about who really is representing biblical Christianity—they or we. But according to God's Word, confusion is one of the great tactics of the enemy. God said that He is never the author of confusion (1 Corinthians 14:33). The purpose of the wolf in sheep's clothing is always to confuse and deceive the sheep to his own gain.

4

A Different Gospel: Way Theology

The apostle Paul clearly warned about those who preach a *different gospel*. He said to the Christians of Galatia: "I am amazed that you are so quickly deserting Him who called you by the grace of Christ, for a different gospel" (Galatians 1:6). He likewise warned the Corinthians not to be deceived by those who preach "another Jesus . . . a different spirit . . . or a different gospel" (2 Corinthians 11:4). It is my contention that Wierwille does just that. Even though he uses the Bible and Christian terminology constantly, plus many of the familiar songs of the faith, in reality he is preaching and teaching a *different gospel* about a *different Jesus,* a gospel that is inspired and empowered by a *different spirit.*

As is the case with every other cult, The Way movement deviates from historic Christianity on the divinity of Christ, the triunity of God, and the Scriptures as the full, complete, and final written revelation of God to man. As I have previously indicated, one will find members of The Way using much of our traditional biblical terminology. However, *even though they use our vocabulary they do not use our dictionary.* In other words, although they may express their doctrine with much of the traditional terminology of orthodox Christians, *they do not mean the same thing by the use of those words or phrases*. So, even though we and they might sound alike, we do not share a common faith with them at all. At least Mr. Wierwille has now forthrightly acknowledged this in writing when he warned his followers that Way people must define their terms lest many who hear them be misled.[1]

According to The Way, the Bible must be clearly and accurately understood. Wierwille claims to do this because of his "over thirty-five years of independent biblical research." It was during that period of his study that he claims to have rediscovered what the original apostles taught, a teaching that was lost to Christianity until he rediscovered it. When asked, "Do you consider yourselves in line with historic Christianity?," one of the Way's leaders answered, "We're not concerned with what somebody else taught." Indeed, the only similarity the followers of The Way see with any group in church history is with the apostolic church of the first century. "There have been very few organizations like us in history that want a perfectly biblical view," said the leader.

The theology of The Way, then, is a strange mixture of various theological and philosophical strands. Let me outline a few of their beliefs before narrowing in on the main areas in which they deviate from orthodox Christianity.

1. Unitarianism: God exists only in one substance and in one person. Christ was, therefore, a *created being;* and the Holy Spirit is not a person, but only divine attributes. There are similarities here to the Jehovah's Witnesses, who likewise believe that Jesus was a created being. The difference between the two groups concerns the time of Christ's beginning. The Jehovah's Witnesses say that Christ was the *first* created being. God first created Christ and then through Him created everything else. The Way, on the other hand, says that Christ was created in the womb of Mary so did not come into being until His birth in Bethlehem. Both groups, then, say that *God alone is eternal* and that *Christ is a created being*.

2. *Biblical literalism:* "The Word of God means what it says and says what it means." That is one of Wierwille's favorite statements. What he really means is this: "The Word of God means what I say and says what I mean." He is the one who has the correct interpretation. So in spite of what Way members say to the contrary, The Way is not a group that is formed around the Bible, but a group that is formed around one man's interpretation of it. Another of Wierwille's pet phrases is "working the Word," which, he maintains, he alone does correctly. This amounts to *bibliolatry,* which is worship of the Bible or one person's interpretation of it rather than worship of its main figure, Jesus Christ. More will be said later about the Bible and The Way.

3. *Salvation by faith:* For The Way, salvation is entirely by grace through faith in the virgin-born, crucified, resurrected, and ascended Son of God. The Way would agree with much of Christian orthodoxy on the facts of the incarnate life of Christ. Where they differ, as I have previously said, is on his *preincarnate* existence.

Concerning salvation, they greatly stress Romans 10:9: "that if you confess with your mouth Jesus as Lord, and believe in your heart that God raised Him from the dead, you shall be saved." Salvation for them is more *confessional,* or *creedal,* than experiential. Again, on the surface it would appear that Wierwille teaches the traditional view of justification by faith. But, we are justified, says Wierwille, not by our faith but by "the faith of Jesus Christ." So according to Wierwille, it is the faith *of* Jesus Christ that saves us—not our faith *in*

Jesus. Wierwille's reasoning for this is that the natural man cannot have faith, only *belief*. Once he believes, he then receives the "faith of Jesus," which in turn saves him. All references to faith before the book of Acts are errors of translation, he says.[2] However, this novel interpretation will not hold up because the words *faith* and *belief* are often used synonymously in the Bible.

4. *Calvinism:* Once a person is saved, he cannot become unsaved. The Way's particular emphasis here causes them to lean toward antinomianism, or lawlessness. Because Christ has paid for all our sins, we are free to do whatever we think is acceptable. This unbalanced emphasis on grace without the balance of morality tends to open the door to license. I was on an overnight flight to Israel with a large number of Way members who freely drank various alcoholic beverages and smoked constantly. This seems somewhat contradictory to their emphasis on physical fitness and health foods, especially because tobacco has definitely been proved injurious to health. I am not seeking to make an issue of drinking or smoking. I am just illustrating a point concerning the freedom they emphasize by continuing to indulge in those kinds of things. I know that not all Christians agree on the badness of smoking and drinking; but we do agree that a Christian must be sensitive both to his witness to the world and to the weaknesses of his brother.

5. *Dispensationalism:* The church began with Paul's epistles. The gospels belong to the Old Testament; and only those New Testament epistles addressed to the church apply to believers today, although the remainder of the Bible is "for our learning."

6. *Pentecostalism:* The nine spiritual gifts of 1 Corinthians are operable today and available to *every* believer. Particular emphasis is placed on tongues and healing.

With that brief outline of The Way's theology, let us turn now to a breakdown of the crucial errors.

48

5

Another Jesus: Christology

Anybody who says Jesus is God is not gonna stand approved before God on that statement, I guarantee ya![1]

God is from everlasting to everlasting. He was before the foundations. He has no beginning, no end . . . His Son had a beginning.[2][Victor Paul Wierwille]

Finally, Mr. Wierwille has said openly and directly what he has been intimating quietly for years: "Jesus Christ is not God." In fact, at 6:00 A.M. on Reformation Sunday, October 30, 1977, Wierwille and about two hundred of his followers posted a document on the door of the First United Church of Christ (New Knoxville), in which he was raised.

Under the heading "Jesus Christ is not God—never was and never will be," Wierwille's document asserted that Jesus is neither God the Son nor a member of the Trinity. He listed more than sixty scripture references that call Him rather the "Son of God." The paper stated that no verse declares Jesus to be God the Son, that Jesus was tempted and that God cannot be, and that Jesus was not omniscient as is God.

In his concluding paragraphs, Wierwille referred to both his Huguenot ancestry and his close association with the New Knoxville church. His own signature headed the list of signers.

After he posted this document—Martin Luther style—to the church door, a *Way Magazine* editorial gave these summary remarks:

> Dr. Wierwille strode back to the custom coach after placing an autographed copy of *Jesus Christ is Not God* at the foot of the church door for all to see. As the custom coach pulled away, its foghorn blasted three times to signify the ceremony's completion—a final symbolic attempt to shatter the complacency enveloping the town.[3]

Wierwille himself made this assessment in a newspaper interview the next day:

> When my life is over I think my greatest contribution may prove to be the knowledge and teaching that Jesus Christ is not God. Before I finish, my life may stir up the biggest beehive in Roman Catholicism and Protestantism since the religious leaders took a shot at Martin Luther. May there be a true reformation in our day and time.[4]

Whether those events will create the kind of theological upheaval that Martin Luther's declaration did remains to be seen. However, those events—along with this book—should go a long way in clearing up any possible misunderstanding of just where The Way stands on this most crucial of all issues in Christianity. Wierwille says, "I am saying that Jesus Christ is not God, but the Son of God. They are not 'co-eternal, without beginning or end, and co-equal.' " He then contends that Jesus was neither with God in the beginning nor does He possess all the "assets" of God.[5]

So Jesus is very important to followers of The Way, but God the Father alone is God.[6] According to Wierwille, none who teach that Jesus is God, or vice versa, will ever stand approved as "rightly dividing" the Scriptures.[7] For Wierwille, then, Jesus is a specially created, perfect man whose body comes from Mary and whose soul, or "life principle," was specially created by God in Mary's womb. Wierwille's reasoning is as follows: Had Jesus been naturally conceived, He would have been a sinner. However (says Wierwille) at His conception those genes that bore the dominant characteristics came by way of divinely created sperm. Thus Jesus was without sin.[8]

In Wierwille's scheme of things, then, it is crucial that Jesus be the only begotten *Son of God* and not *God the Son*. He believes that for man to be redeemed, it is essential that the Redeemer be man and not God.[9]

Christ, then, is seen by Wierwille as having been uniquely created by a form of divine insemination; so He was born sinless. He was, therefore, able to die for the sins of the world as the "only begotten son" of the Father, who alone is God. I once heard Wierwille stress the phrase "only begotten Son" in seeking to validate his position in his book *Jesus Christ Is Not God*; his statement was: "It says 'For God so loved the world that He gave his only *begotten* Son. . . .' It doesn't say 'For God so loved the world that He gave God.' " Wierwille then slapped the pulpit and laughed as he said: "Read it and don't bug me on it! If this cuts across your theology, I'm sorry!"[10]

What he says does not so much cut across orthodoxy's opinion or theology as it does across the revealed Word of God. The expression "only begotten Son" clearly teaches the deity of Christ. The Greek root word for "only begotten" is the word *monogenes*. With the exception of Luke 7:12; 8:42; 9:38, and Hebrews 11:17, it occurs in the New Testament only in the writings of John (John 1:14, 18; 3:16, 18; 1 John 4:9), and then it is used only in reference to Christ. As M. R. Vincent says:

> John's word marks the relation to the Father as unique. . . . [*Monogenes*] distinguishes between Christ as the *only* Son, . . . the only Son did not *become* . . . such by receiving power, by adoption, or by moral generation, but *was* . . . such in the beginning with God. The fact set forth does not belong to the sphere of His incarnation, but of His eternal being.[11]

So, the word here for "only begotten" clearly does not imply beginning as applied to an ordinary man; it means *unoriginated relationship,* a fact irrespective of time. John is thus saying that Christ did not *become* the Son ("the Word") but rather eternally *is* the Son. He is expressing Christ's pre-existence and eternal union with the Father and Spirit in the Godhead. The biblical revelation through John then is that Jesus Christ did not become the only begotten Son at the incarnation. *The incarnation only gave expression in time to what He eternally is in the Godhead.* Wierwille says that at His birth in Bethlehem, Jesus became the only begotten Son of God—at that point He came into existence. But the Bible teaches that His incarnation in Bethlehem gave expression in time to what Jesus had eternally pre-existed as—God the Son.

Although the followers of Wierwille like to think of themselves as "holding forth the accuracy of God's Word," they are actually only repeating one of the oldest heresies of the church in a slightly modernized form. Ecclesiastes 1:9 states: "There is nothing new under the sun." Victor Paul Wierwille and The Way are verifications of the truth of this biblical statement in the theological realm. Wierwille is stressing one of the oldest of

Christian heresies, namely, the unity of God at the expense of His diversity as three Persons.

When Wierwille claims no originality for much of his teaching, he speaks correctly.[12] As any student of church history knows, his heretical teachings have been around for a long time. In the third century, Paul of Samosata, bishop of Antioch from 260 to 272, taught essentially the same doctrine. At that time the heresy was called "Dynamic Monarchianism" and those who professed such a doctrine were called "Monarchians," a title coined by Tertullian—champion of orthodoxy of that day—because those of this persuasion compared God to a divine monarch.* It is interesting that Wierwille also compares God to a monarch. Basically, Paul of Samosata held that Jesus was the Son of God by adoption; thus he was called an "adoptionist." Wierwille, on the other hand, says that Christ became the Son of God by divine artificial insemination. So we could perhaps call Wierwille an "inseminationist."

Many young couples in our culture are unable to have children because of a biological male deficiency. The traditional approach to obtaining a child under those conditions has been through adoption. Some, however, go through the process of artificially inseminating the wife. Thus, artificial insemination is a substitute for adoption. Wierwille has taken this modern idea and adapted it to traditional adoptionism, which often had Christ being "adopted" by God at His baptism. Christ is not the "adopted Son," says Wierwille, but the miracu-

---

*The Monarchians were those in the second and third centuries who opted for a unipersonal rather than a trinitarian view of the divine nature. They did so to preserve the unity of God. In this view, Jesus is regarded as a unique man who was divinely energized by the Holy Spirit—at His baptism, according to the usual belief—and thereby called to be the Son of God [Samuel J. Mikolaski, "Monarchianism." In *The New International Dictionary of the Christian Church*, edited by J. D. Douglas (Grand Rapids: Zondervan, 1974), p.670].

lously (virgin birth) inseminated Son who was given only dominant "sinless" genes. So, even though Wierwille is somewhat more sophisticated and, perhaps, better at attempting to deal with the sinlessness of Christ's nature, he and Paul of Samosata are saying essentially the same thing—Jesus Christ is not God, but the Son of God. In adopting this position, Wierwille simply joins the ranks of earlier heretics like Paul of Samosata, Marcion, Saturninus, Montanus, and Arius. All these men were condemned by the church as heretics and "dispoilers of the flock of Christ."[13]

If Christ is not God but a creation of God, then to worship Him is idolatry. Therefore, however much Wierwille might love and adore Christ, he does not worship Him. Concerning this, he cites the first commandment, "Thou shalt have no other gods before me" (Exodus 20:3).[14]

The Way, then, is not really a form of Christianity, because its followers do not accept the deity of Christ or worship Him as the second Member of the Triune Godhead. This is very confusing to the uninitiated because of all of Wierwille's talk about Jesus as the "Son of God" and His important role as "Mediator" or "Redeemer."

As Christians, we would want to ask Wierwille: What did Christ mean when He said, "He who has seen Me has seen the Father" (John 14:9)? Wierwille would say that Jesus is the highest form of communication—a "concrete form"—from God to man. Jesus is only a visible expression of God to man. Wierwille, then, has God manifesting His will to man in different forms, and there is essentially no difference between the *Word* (the Bible), the *Son* (Christ), and the *Holy Spirit* (the gift of God); all three form a sort of subtrinity manifesting the will of God to man.

Where was Jesus Christ before He was born to Mary?

asks Wierwille. He was nonexistent except in the foreknowledge of God is his own reply:

> Jesus Christ was with God in His foreknowledge.
> . . . "Jesus Christ was with God before the foun-
> dation of the world, meaning that God foreknew
> Him. . . . When Jesus Christ was born, he came
> into existence. Foreknowledge became a real-
> ity."[15]

Trying to prove his theory, Wierwille quotes 1 Peter
1:20: "For He was foreknown before the foundation of
the world, but has appeared in these last times for the
sake of you." The word Peter used there for "fore-
know" is *proginosko*. It means "to know before" (*pro*
means "before"; *ginosko* means "to know"). Wierwille
says that it was the concept, or idea, of Christ—*not the
person*—that was known to the Father before the foundation of the world. But again, Wierwille did not do his
Greek homework. The word *ginosko* indicates a relationship between the one who knows and the one who is
known. It is the same word used in Matthew 1:25 and
Luke 1:34 of the intimate relationship between a man and
a woman. So, contrary to Wierwille's interpretation,
Christ did not come into being at His conception in the
womb of the virgin Mary. Neither did his birth give
expression to some nonexistent foreknowledge of God.
His "appearing," as Peter called it, gave expression to
what He eternally had been before that time: pre-existent
with the Father.

Several other references from *Jesus Christ Is Not God*
will further clarify Mr. Wierwille's teaching concerning
Jesus Christ. He asserts that those who hold that Jesus is
God and God is Jesus use isolated scripture verses to
substantiate their view.[16]

Contrary to that statement, there are scores of Bible
texts that clearly teach the deity of Christ. Wierwille acts
as though he lists and refutes them all in his book. In

reality, he does neither. He does not come close to dealing with all the verses that teach the deity of Christ. The ones he does deal with he treats very superficially. He approaches each one with his preconceived ideas and then seeks to "work the Word," as he calls it, until it seems to support his theology. Some of his argument sounds good to the biblical babe who may be deceived and convinced by his use of Greek or Aramaic and his "exegesis" of Scripture. However, to a more mature Bible student or language scholar, it is a travesty.

Obviously, those who challenge the deity of Christ must face innumerable difficult passages of Scripture—far too many to deal with in this book. So I shall only deal with several, any of which is conclusive. First there is John 1:1-18—the prologue to John's gospel. In it John clearly sets forth by revelation three aspects of the person of Christ: (1) His true deity; (2) His true humanity; and (3) the unity of His person. Realizing the importance of this passage, Wierwille devotes a whole chapter of his book *Jesus Christ Is Not God* to trying to make it agree with his presuppositions. In that chapter, Wierwille's basic approach to circumventing John 1 is to assert that the *Word,* or Jesus, was not "in the beginning" with God as part of the Godhead, as John writes. Instead, Christ was pre-existent with the Father in the same way that the written Word was pre-existent with the Father—in His foreknowledge.[17]

He says further that the issue in John 1:1 is who or what is "the Word."[18] His answer to that is that the Father—not Jesus—is the *logos,* or "Word," of John 1:1. Wierwille further says that only the second usage of "the Word" in John 1:1 refers to Christ; the first and third usages refer to God. Thus we have Wierwille's "literal translation" of John 1:1-2:

In the beginning (before the creation) God was the

Word, and the revealed Word was in God's foreknowledge (which was later communicated to man
in spoken Words, written Words and the incarnate
Word). This Word absolutely was in the beginning
before the foundation of the world together with
the one true God in His foreknowledge yet dis-
tinctly independent of Him.[19]

That rendering obviously violates the clear intent of
the passage. Nowhere in the history of the biblical
exegesis of the prologue to John's gospel has *logos* ever
been defined the way Wierwille has sought to define it.
His misuse of the Greek here is again blatant. All
through the prologue, John uses the same basic verbal
form, the imperfect† form of the verb "to be." That
form of that verb stresses the continuous existence of
something in past time. So in essence John is saying:
"When the beginning was, the Word was continuously
existing face to face with God, and the Word was continuously such a one as God." The true thrust of the verb
here, then, is on the continuousness of the existence of
Christ in past times. Contrary to Wierwille's teaching
that Christ came into being at His conception in the
womb of Mary, John actually is saying: *"When the beginning was, Christ was continuously existing."*

John 1:3 clearly says that the Word, Jesus, was eternal, inasmuch as everything created came into being
through Him.

Wierwille goes on to describe creation, life, and light
in verses 3 through 5 as all referring to God and not the
Word. He continues in the prologue and says that John
came to bear witness to God, not Christ (vv. 6-9). John
1:10 poses another problem. Here John says, "He was in
the world, and the world was made through Him, and the

---

†The imperfect tense in the Greek denotes action in progress, or a state
existing, in past time with no view to its beginning or ending.

world did not know Him." By a carefully linked chain, Wierwille "shows" the subject here to be "God" and not "the Word" from verses 1 and 2. Then between verses 12 and 13, Mr. Wierwille makes a shift—and it is obvious why. If the subject in verse 12 is God and in verse 13 God is born, that is, becomes Christ, then Christ becomes someone more than the Son of God as Wierwille defines Him. Therefore, Wierwille "translates" verse 12 as follows:

> But as many [of Israel] as received Him [God], to them gave He [God] power [*exousia,* authority, the right] to become the sons of God, *even* to them that believe on [unto] his name [namesake, Jesus Christ] (brackets Wierwille's).[20]

Wierwille's inconsistency in ascribing "name" to Christ is glaring.

Finally, in verse 18 John summarizes his prologue. "No man has seen God at any time; the only begotten God, who is in the bosom of the Father, He has explained Him." Concerning this verse, as previously noted, Wierwille teaches that Christ was in the Father's bosom in "foreknowledge" only. As Mr. John Weldon, a former research assistant to Dr. Walter Martin and author of several cult-related books, said to me in a letter: "It is obvious that Wierwille is having to place his presuppositions upon the text and then push or outright pervert meanings of words." I would point out that *nowhere is the word* foreknowledge *used in the biblical text.* It specifically says, "The Word was God." The subject of verses 1 through 5 is clearly the Word, or Jesus Christ—*not* God the Father. As in verses 6 through 8, John is bearing witness specifically to "the Word," which is described in verse 5 as "light." So it is evident that verses 9 through 13 also refer to Christ. Finally, verse 14 clearly establishes Christ as the eternally begotten, pre-incarnate Word when it states: "And the Word became flesh."‡

Wierwille definitely denies the pre-existence of Christ and, therefore, sees Him as a created being of exalted position—but not deity—and certainly not the second Person of the Trinity. This is very similar to the position held by the Jehovah's Witnesses and Unitarians. Here, then is the *created* Jesus Christ of Victor Paul Wierwille and The Way: Jesus Christ, it is asserted, began to exist when God created the sperm, with its soul-life, that impregnated Mary.[21]

CONCLUSIONS

Rather than the Christ of the Bible and history, Wierwille's Jesus is definitely "another Jesus," a Christ like the ones Paul warned about in his letters to both the Corinthian and Galatian Christians. Wierwille's Christ is a Christ who cannot save, because He is not fully God and fully man. For Christ to be a bridge between man and God, He *must,* like a physical bridge, be firmly established on both shores. Otherwise the chasm that separates man from God would not be bridged. We would have no mediator. And we would still be lost in our sins. But thanks be to God, Jesus eternally was and is what the Bible and the church councils have declared Him to be: the unique God-Man of history.

---

‡For a good further refutation of Mr. Wierwille's interpretation of John 1:1-18—plus all other such slanted exegesis, consult *Was Christ God?*, by Spiros Zodhiates (Grand Rapids: Eerdmans, 1966).

6

Ancient Heresy Revived

Here is how an advertisement for Wierwille's book *Jesus Christ Is Not God* read in a Way magazine: "Trinitarian dogma placing Jesus Christ on God's level degrades God and leaves man UNREDEEMED! A product of 33 years of Biblical research by Dr. Victor Paul Wierwille."[1]

What has been the response to the revival of this ancient Arian heresy by Wierwille? Here is his evaluation: "From those who have not been steeped in wrong theological background who were men and women of great potential of logical thinking, the response has been fantastic, and it's growing daily!"[2] Wierwille is even convinced that Martin Luther would have agreed with his conclusions:

> If Martin Luther'd have had more time, and lived in our culture, perhaps, I'm confident he would have come up with a far better work on *Jesus Christ Is Not God* than I did, 'cause he knew it. But he just didn't have time.[3]

Again, I have to call Wierwille's hand on his lack of

historical homework. Martin Luther never would have agreed with Wierwille. He did in fact live long enough to write a far better work, but it did not say that Jesus Christ is not God. It declared the truth that Jesus Christ *is* God. In 1529, Martin Luther wrote a catechism in which he stated that Jesus is "true God and true man." Arius of Alexandria, Paul of Samosata, Marcion, Saturnius, Montanus, and other such heretics would have agreed with Wierwille, but never Martin Luther. Wierwille's teachings about Christ's not being God would have been complete anathema to him.

WIERWILLE'S BLUFF IS CALLED

Wierwille seems so sure of himself in stating that Jesus is not God that he says he is ready to defend the statement publicly in debate:

> Have you got a public platform you'd like to put this on and finance it? . . . an international discussion, nationally and internationally televised, on Jesus Christ, God's Son. And the other side where we say that He is the Son of God and protestantism says He is God. . . . I'm ready . . . to take on any theologian, any group of scholars, any place in the whole world. One testbook, the Word.

> Now I've got other scholars in The Way ministry, better scholars, perhaps, than even I am. I never said I am a scholar. Never said that in my life, but I know I got a few . . . I've got other men that can handle it from a lot of different angles and substantiate it eight, nine, ten more times than what I substantiated it in the book.[4]

However, the more he talks the less sure you are who will show up—Wierwille or someone else:

> We'll handle it. Any place, in any theological field. And I'll—I won't even handle it, I'll have

one of my students handle it. I'm no longer going to go up before this stuff. I don't care. I got young men that can handle it.[5]

So when pushed into a corner, he changes his position. Through letters and conversations, I have personally challenged Wierwille and others of his leaders to a public debate on the issue. Here is the written response I received:

"A man convinced against his will is of the same opinion still." This quotation is one that I have found to be very true in my experience in the ministry. This, I believe, is definitely true concerning our "getting together" to discuss "biblical principles of exegesis" and is also why I know our meeting public or private would truly not be fruitful. I say this because I believe you have in mind eventually or totally discussing points on which we disagree. Obviously, this would not be "getting together", but would only aid in keeping us apart, which is exactly what our spiritual adversary glories in even at this present time. Frankly, I don't have time for this type of argumentative vanity, and if I don't, I can assure you that Dr. Wierwille doesn't either.[6]

So now Wierwille says: "I don't want to argue. . . . I have no time to argue or fight."[7] But my challenge—and similar ones by many other Christians around the country—still stands. We call his bluff!

Poor Documentation

Wierwille's book *Jesus Christ Is Not God*, like his other books, is a poorly documented work. It is filled with statements, as are his teachings, that are not substantiated or documented. Phrases like the following abound in his writings and teachings:

It would not have been difficult for scribes to insert. . . . This must have been what happened.[8]

The original text probably read . . .[9]

An earlier text must have had a rendering of . . . [10]

Wierwille also gives this account of how John 1:18 was changed from "only begotten Son" to "only begotten God" in some ancient manuscripts. A scribe, he says, who had copied "the only begotten of the Father" in verse 14, might "easily" have carried over the same thought into verse 18, making it read "the only begotten of God." That in turn would later have been changed to "the only begotten God."

However, Wierwille says the alteration *could* have been intentional because of doctrinal error being set forth.[11]

Note that documentation is lacking. He uses phrases like, "The majority of uncials," but he does not cite *any* documentation. He constantly uses words like "could have," "must have," "might," "probably," and so on. I have to ask him for certainties—not subjunctives. When one is tampering with a doctrine on which your salvation rests, he had better be dealing with absolute proof and certainty, not possibilities and probabilities. The reason Wierwille has to work so hard on John 1:18 is because if it is correct, then he is absolutely wrong. What John actually says is this: "No man has seen God at any time; the only begotten God, who is in the bosom of the Father, He has explained Him."

When Wierwille was asked about a number of such verses, verses that he did not deal with adequately in his book and that clearly teach the pre-existence of Christ and, therefore, His deity, he said:

I'll stand with my book. And we'll come back to one more principle. You got one scripture, I got ninety-nine. So you're gonna throw out the ninety-nine and hold to your one. Not me. I just happen to be a scientist and logical enough—I'll go with what I wrote in the book and that's all I'm gonna say about it.[12]

That hardly sounds like the statement of a "scientist" and "logical" thinker. It sounds more like someone who is begging the question. Besides, as we shall see in the following section, he does not have ninety-nine verses to prove his position as opposed to only one for orthodox Christianity. When the Bible is correctly interpreted, orthodoxy has a hundred and Wierwille has none. In essence, his book's arguments and "biblical interpretations" are all testimony to a basic philosophical truth that says: If a man's presuppositions are faulty, his logical conclusions will only serve to magnify the original errors as he extends his argument.

Despite Wierwille's statements about "unpreconceived research," "objectivity," and "unbiasedness," his presupposition is clear: There does not exist the possibility of the Triune Godhead. It is a basic law of logic that your presuppositions automatically predetermine your conclusions. Therefore, when his true presupposition—regardless of what he says to the contrary—is that the Trinity cannot be, then he must likewise explain away the deity of Christ and the Person of the Holy Spirit. He has no alternative. However, to do so he must literally make both history and the text of the Bible say just what he wants them to say. I must agree with the Reverend Mr. Scott Smith, a graduate of Westminster Theological Seminary with an emphasis in biblical languages, who reported this to me after he had read *Jesus Christ Is Not God*: "It is historically slanted, theologically naive, and exegetically a travesty!"

It is truly unfortunate for The Way that Wierwille has filled his book with references to his "years of study," "research," and "checking of God's Word hundreds of times over" during his "personal quest" for the truth about God's Son. For in seeking to impress us with the *quantity* of his research, he forces us to question the *quality* of it when we are told that the book reflects the gleanings of such an "in-depth study."

In the first chapter, "The Origin of the Three-In-One God," Wierwille seeks to trace the origin of the Christian belief in a Triune Godhead to the Babylonians, Hindus, Greeks, and other pagan nations whose religions seem to exhibit a similar belief in a divine triad. His argument is that after the death of the apostles, strong doctrinal emphasis disappeared. The religious and cultural influences of antiquity began to seep into the church in the first four centuries and take their toll on the purity of the gospel. The result was, he claims, that through political pressure applied by Constantine, the heretical promoters of the Trinity won the theological battle in spite of the valiant fight by Arius to maintain the truth.

In taking this stand against the Trinity, Wierwille, in keeping with his liberal Bible training, has adopted the methodology of higher criticism. One of the cardinal tenets of higher criticism is to deny that anything in biblical theology is original, or revealed from God. Everything is believed to have been borrowed from the religions that antedated Christianity by several hundred years.

However, Wierwille has created a problem for himself here. If he is right in saying that the church was influenced by the Babylonian concept of a Trinity, then he for the sake of consistency must also say that much of the Word of God was borrowed from the Babylonians. You see, the Babylonians also had a doctrine of creation, *Enuma elish,* which antedated the Genesis account of the Fall of man, and an account of the flood that parallels in many ways the Genesis account. All these written (cuneiform) accounts of the Babylonians antedated the Bible records by several centuries. Are we, then, to say that the authors of Scripture borrowed those foundational doctrines in the same way that the early church fathers borrowed the doctrine of the Trinity? If we use Wierwille's argument of the religious and cultural influence of pagan antiquity on the origin of the Trinity, we must also conclude, simply because there are accounts that parallel Old Testament stories and that antedated the biblical records, that many of the great doctrines of our faith are syncretisms of ancient pagan beliefs and Christ's teaching. Orthodoxy obviously repudiates such an interpretation.

Wierwille further suggests that the doctrine of the Trinity emerged as Christian converts from paganism sought to maintain some of their old pagan ideologies about a triadic god. However, church history reveals the direct opposite to be true. *The necessity to formulate the doctrine of the Trinity was in response to the threat of pagan theology and not as a result of it.* True, the doctrinal formulas of the early church are not equal to divine revelation. Doctrinal statements always fall short of the reality they are seeking to describe. Nowhere is that more true than when we are seeking to describe God in creedal form. As C. S. Lewis said: "Doctrines are not God: they are only a kind of map. But that map is based on the experience of hundreds of people who really were in touch with God."[13] The men who formulated those creeds of the church were men who were in touch with God. They were not making new statements about God that were contrary to the biblical revelation. They were simply giving labels and putting into creedal form previously existing realities and revelations. We may, therefore, say more about God than the creeds say—but we dare not say less.

In his books and lectures, Wierwille loves to pit the titles of "God" and "Son of God" against each other. His a priori assumption is that they are mutually exclusive terms. He constantly seeks to prove his point by saying:

> John 3:16, what does it say? "For God so loved the World that He sent His only begotten Son." Okay, that's all the further you need to go. Did He give Himself, or did He give what? His Son! That's what it means.[14]

Again, I must say that his exegesis is enslaved to his preconceived conclusions. This is a common interpretation and semantics game played by the other Arian cults—the Mormons, Jehovah's Witnesses, Christian Scientists, and so on. The Bible has a number of antinomies. An antinomy is an apparent contradiction between two equally valid principles, such as the sovereignty of God and the free will of man. On the surface they seem to be contradictory; how can man have free will and God be sovereign? That is an antinomy. They are both revealed truths, and to try to pit them against each other results in doctrinal confusion. The same is true when it comes to the Trinity and the deity of Christ. It would appear to human reason that the oneness and the threeness of God are contradictory. It would also appear that "God" and "Son of God" are mutually exclusive. But in both cases they are clearly revealed truths, truths that must be simultaneously held. We fall into heresy when we seek to hold either one without the other. In so doing we also elevate human reasoning to the throne of omniscience and ultimately say that anything that the human mind cannot fully comprehend must be rejected. Again, that is a confusion of the Creator-creature distinction. Any God that we could fully comprehend would not be a God big enough to worship.

So in spite of Wierwille's desperate attempts to explain away the Trinity and the deity of Christ in his book *Jesus Christ Is Not God,* he does not succeed. Whenever he does appear to be successful in his attempts, a little digging reveals his historical slant and forced interpretation. Again, his exegesis, or biblical interpretation, is enslaved to his preconceived conclusions. One just cannot preconceive or presuppose or define a reality out of existence. And the biblical revelation about the nature of Jesus Christ is that *Jesus, the Son of God, is God.*

7

The Way and the Trinity

> If you have three gods you might as well have
> 3,000 since having more than one is already wrong
> according to the Bible.
>
> Victor Paul Wierwille[1]

Before you can begin fully to understand Wierwille's
doctrine of the Holy Spirit, which is the subject of a
following chapter, you must first understand what he
believes about the Trinity. It is not surprising that if he
does not believe that Jesus is God, then neither does he
believe that the Holy Spirit is God. That means that if
neither the Son nor the Spirit is God, then there is no
Godhead, no Trinity. That is exactly what Wierwille
teaches:

> Christianity never had three gods. We've only got
> one. And that one God is manifested, as it says, in
> His Son, Jesus Christ. . . . If Jesus Christ was God,
> and God died on the cross, the teaching that God is

dead is right, sir. Then who raised God from the dead if God died on the cross? You see, man's mind is so tricky. His logic blows my mind! They cannot add two plus two spiritually. They can do it in math; when it comes to God's Word, they can't track![2]

That is Wierwille's logic concerning the Trinity. Apparently the doctrine had always troubled him in his earlier life and ministry. He says that as he studied the Bible, he entertained the hope that he would find the key to an understanding of the Trinity. He goes on to say that he had asked theologians to discuss the subject with him.[3] Wierwille has evidently convinced himself that he has objectively and thoroughly studied the subject. "I think I've read everything that's ever been written that is in existence that I know of on the Trinity, all the theological works, everything else, and I suppose I have a two-foot file on just that phase of teaching alone."[4] Wierwille says that none of his study and research was motivated by a desire to refute trinitarian doctrine.[5] That motivation has now clearly changed, however, because Wierwille goes to great lengths to try to disprove the doctrine of the Trinity, as we shall soon see.

If the doctrine of the Trinity is not revealed in the Bible, we must ask, Where did it come from? Here is Wierwille's answer:

> You got the Trinity out of Babylonian paganism, baptized by Roman Catholicism, and indoctrinated in the hearts and lives of the Occident (Western) theologians down through Europe, down through America. Never was any Trinity, you know, in the Christendom stuff, until that third-century business came along.[6]

Trinitarianism, then, according to Wierwille, is baptized paganism.

WIERWILLE, CHURCH HISTORY, AND HERESY

That "third-century business," as Wierwille called it, was the famous Council of Nicaea held in 325. The first chapter of *Jesus Christ Is Not God* gives his account of it as well as his interpretation of the events that surrounded it.

Wierwille claims that the doctrine of the Trinity, having evolved from pagan religions, was given official acceptance by churchmen for political reasons. The trinitarian doctrine was not held by the first-century church. Rather, the teaching developed as converted pagans brought into the church certain pagan beliefs and practices during the first three centuries of the Christian era.[7]

Wierwille then asserts that although the confirmation of trinitarianism at Nicaea was a political move, the doctrine has since been adhered to as if it had been revealed by God.[8] That statement is a sham of scholarship. If space permitted, literally hundreds of pages of quotations by "historians of Church dogma and systematic theologians"—to use his words—could be given to disprove his statement. To answer this allegation brings one close to giving "answer [to] a fool according to his folly" (Proverbs 26:4). However, because many people are accepting Wierwille's statement as the result of true scholarship, I must briefly answer it.

He first seeks to show that many of the great theological heroes of the church are in reality the culprits who perpetuated the Trinitarian heresy. Men such as Irenaeus, Tertullian, Cyprian, and Augustine are seen as the real enemies of the correct doctrine of God. To Wierwille, Arius of Alexandria was the theological hero of the day. Wierwille claims that no one in all the first three centuries of church history believed that Jesus Christ is God or believed in the doctrine of the Trinity. "This is an odd contention," says Jack Sparks, "since Irenaeus was living in 160 A.D., Tertullian in 200 A.D., and Cyprian in 250 A.D.!"[9] Wierwille's recounting of history is again found lacking.

Wierwille also says the council was composed of about two hundred twenty bishops, almost all from the Western Church[10] Again he is either misinformed or guilty of misrepresenting the facts. In reality some 318 bishops were present, not to mention the more than fifteen hundred other bishops, elders, and deacons who were also there. And, contrary again to what Wierwille says, it was not a one-sided council that was "almost exclusively from the Occident." As the *New International Dictionary of the Christian Church* says: "The council was hardly representative of the Western (Occident) Church. Of some 300 bishops present, almost all were from the Eastern half of the empire."[11] So, contrary to Wierwille's interpretation of the events, the Nicaean council was not a Western-dominated affair and the doctrine of the Trinity was not a Western theological bias. Bishops and representatives were there from all over the Christian world. As F.F. Bruce says: "The Council, which met at Nicaea in north-west Asia Minor on May 20, 325, was the first ecumenical council of the Church; that is to say, the first to which representatives were called from churches all over the known world."[12]

Wierwille would also have us believe that the creed that was signed there was the achievement of a minority.[13] In reality, only two of the over three hundred bishops present refused to sign the creed, and "they were forthwith excommunicated, along with Arius himself."[14]

Finally, Wierwille tries to convince his readers that those who did sign at Nicaea did so only because of pressure from Constantine. Again he is guilty of misrepresenting the facts. It takes a real stretch of the imagination to believe that a group of bishops like those at

Nicaea could be frightened or intimidated by Constantine. Many of them had already gone through the fires of persecution for their faith in the deity of Christ. They certainly would not submit to heresy for Constantine. As Jack Sparks rightly says about the Council of Nicaea:

> There was indeed some "overawe" there, but it wasn't from the bishops. It was Constantine, the emperor, who was overawed. He'd never seen such a group of men in all his life. There were those there who had gone through some of the most terrifying persecutions imaginable at the hands of the Roman Empire.
>
> Some had empty socket where their eyes had been before they had been gouged out by torturers because they refused to renounce their faith in Jesus Christ. Others had had members of their bodies cut off. Still others had been augered—giant drill bits had been drilled into their arms and legs and other parts of their bodies, because they wouldn't deny Christ.
>
> Constantine had never seen such commitment, or devotion, or dedication to anyone. He was so moved that he walked about the assembly and kissed the scars of these heroic confessors. (That's what they called those who had suffered because they preferred to be tortured rather than renounce Christ.)[15]

I have to agree totally with Sparks's conclusions: "And we are to assume from Wierwille that the men who met at Nicaea were spineless men who were snookered into signing a creed in which they did not believe, because of overawe and political expediency!!?? What garbage!"[16]

Again, I have to say that Wierwille is guilty of either very sloppy historical research, gross misrepresentation of the facts, or both. That is a tragedy in and of itself. But a far greater tragedy is that his story is being read

75

and believed by thousands as accurate historical and biblical research. I am often reminded of the maxim that says the one who does not remember the past is condemned to repeat it! So this misrepresentation of Wierwille's is being believed by scores of young people simply because they have never studied the facts of church history for themselves.

The doctrine of the Trinity is revealed clearly in the Bible (see Appendix 2) and confirmed by the councils of church history. It is Wierwille's opinion that is heretical.

WIERWILLE'S STRAW IMAGE

Not only does Wierwille misrepresent the Council of Nicaea historically, but he also misrepresents the doctrine of the Trinity theologically. Wierwille starts out his discussions of the doctrine of the Trinity by setting up a straw man. He says that Christians who believe in the Trinity believe in and worship three gods. Again, that is either a total misunderstanding of the doctrine on his part, a purposeful misrepresentation, or both. Christianity never has believed in three gods. That is tritheism (*tri* means "three"; *theism* means "god"), which is a form of polytheism (*poly* means "many"), and that is paganism from the Christian standpoint. Christianity believes in one God who eternally exists as Father, Son, and Holy Spirit. There is a triunity in the Godhead. C.S. Lewis illustrated this three-in-oneness: "In God's dimension, so to speak, you find a being who is three Persons while remaining one Being, just as a cube is six squares while remaining one cube."[17] So Trinitarianism is not tritheism, and Wierwille should know better than to confuse the two.

Wierwille thus begins his discussion of the Trinity by misrepresenting the doctrine. Setting up a straw image of the doctrine of the Trinity and then destroying it is not scholarship. What he defeats is not the true doctrine but a misrepresentation of it.

I will quickly admit that neither you nor I nor Wierwille can ever fully comprehend the mystery of the Trinity. If we could, we would be the fourth member of the Trinity! God cannot be totally comprehended by man. The finite can never totally comprehend the Infinite. That is why the triunity of God is a *revealed* truth. Man's reason could never attain it. It is a revelation that goes *beyond* reason—but not *against* it. It was Augustine who said that you could spend your life trying to understand the Trinity and in the process lose your mind. "But deny it," he said, "and you will lose your soul."

Christianity, then, and its revelation about the nature of God, has the ring of truth to it. C.S. Lewis said:

> Reality, in fact, is usually something you could not have guessed. That is one of the reasons I believe Christianity. It is a religion you could not have guessed. . . . it is not the sort of thing anyone would have made up. It has just that queer twist about it that real things have. . . . It is something we could never have guessed, and yet, once we have been told, one almost feels one ought to have been able to guess it because it fits in so well with all the things we know already.[18]

BAPTIZED PAGANISM

As we saw in the previous section about Nicaea, Wierwille would have us believe that Constantine forced the church bishops to adopt the Trinitarian position so that Christianity would mix better with the paganism of the empire. He tries to prove that the existence in pre-Christian religions of some form of triad of gods is the origin of the Christian doctrine of the Trinity.

Belief in a triune god, Wierwille asserts, was common among ancient religions. Brahma, Vishu, and Shiva composed the Hindu trinity. That of the Greeks was made up of Zeus, Athena, and Apollo. The Roman trinity was of Jupiter, Mercury, and Venus. In Babylon, Venus, the moon, and the sun were revered as a trinity.[19]

Again I am surprised that Wierwille's study and resulting representation are so shallow and distorted. My master's degree work was done in the field of comparative world religions. I can confidently say that Wierwille just has not done his homework in this area either. It is certainly true that other cultures and religions before the Christian era had a concept of three gods who appear to form some sort of trinity. The Hindus, Greeks, and Romans had a three-god triad, but those did not come close to the Christian doctrine of the Trinity. Those cultures and religions had a three-god concept, but the members of their divine triads were not co-equal and co-eternal. Neither did they share the same nature and essence. They also did not have a perfect unity among them. In fact, the opposite was true. They were often seen as battling and warring among themselves, each trying to outdo the others. There are passions and jealous rages between them at times. Their three gods were a form of tritheism, with three distinct and different persons, or gods. And, as we have already seen, tritheism is not trinitarianism. Please remember that important distinction. Tritheism is a belief in three distinct gods, whereas trinitarianism is a belief in three Persons, but one God.

Also, most of those other religions did not stop with their belief in three chief gods. They often had hundreds—even thousands—of lesser gods who were all vying for power and influence.

So Wierwille seems bothered by the fact that we find a hint, or prelude, of the concept of the Trinity in other religions. Tritheism, as we have seen, is not trinitarianism—but it "hints" at it. It is what we might call a pagan distortion of trinitarianism. As Wierwille says, the concept of a triune God is deeply rooted in human thinking. I believe that that is true for a very good and obvious reason. The concept is part of that light that "enlightens every man" (John 1:9). When we understand the true nature of God and His love for man, is it not to be expected that He would place within every man something of a knowledge of Himself? Is that not part of Paul's argument in Romans when he says:

> For the wrath of God is revealed from heaven against all ungodliness and unrighteousness of men, who suppress the truth in unrighteousness, because that which is known about God is evident within them; for God made it evident to them [Romans 1:18-19].

Paul not only says that this knowledge of God is "evident within them," but he also says that God's "invisible attributes, His eternal power and divine nature, have been clearly seen, being understood through what has been made" (Romans 1:20).

As C.S. Lewis said: "If you are a Christian you do not have to believe that all the other religions are simply wrong all through. . . . If you are a Christian, you are free to think that all these religions, even the queerest ones, contain at least some hint of the truth."[20] So in reality, some similarities between certain Christian doctrines and those found in other religions are to be expected. In fact, they constitute a kind of proof for Christianity. *The counterfeit always testifies to the existence of the real.* If Christianity were totally different in every way from all the world religions, one would become suspicious. Lewis put it this way in another of his books:

> I couldn't believe that nine-hundred and ninety-nine religions were completely false and the re-

maining one true. In reality, Christianity is primarily the fulfilment of the Jewish religion, but also the fulfilment of what was vaguely hinted in all the religions at their best. What was vaguely seen in them all comes into focus in Christianity—just as God Himself comes into focus by becoming a Man.[21]

I concur with Lewis's conclusions rather than Wierwille's, saying that "we are not pronouncing all other religions to be totally false, but rather saying that in Christ whatever is true in all religions is consummated and perfected."[22]

So we should expect to find hinted in pre-Christian religions what we find being perfectly revealed in Christianity. That includes the doctrine of the Trinity.

8

Another Spirit: Pneumatology

In the holy spirit field, our piece of research is the
most thorough and original coverage of the subject.

Victor Paul Wierwille[1]

Wierwille's chief book that sets forth his doctrine of
the Holy Spirit is *Receiving the Holy Spirit Today*.

As we have already seen, Wierwille's basic concept is
that God is one in substance and only one in person. We
have seen that this forces him to deny the deity of Christ.
Let us now apply this understanding of God to the Holy
Spirit.

As previously noted, Wierwille agrees with the
Jehovah's Witnesses that the doctrine of the Trinity is
contrary to the Scriptures. To him, the Holy Spirit is the
Father (God) by another name, just as Dick and Richard
can be two names for the same person. One follower of
The Way expressed it to me this way: "God is holy and
God is spirit, but the Holy Spirit is not God."

As is often the case, Wierwille tries to substantiate his
doctrine of the Holy Spirit and the Trinity by a facade of

scholarship, or "biblical research." See "Wierwille, Church History, and Heresy" in chapter 7.

WIERWILLE'S HOLY SPIRIT

Mr. Wierwille, therefore, believes that the Holy Spirit is a synonym for God the Father—not a person distinct from the Father.* He says that God is holy (*hagion*) and God is spirit (*pneuma*); therefore, it is correct to say that God is holy spirit. But the Holy Spirit is not a person distinct from God the Father in the Godhead. The Holy Spirit is just another name for God.

To follow Wierwille's reasoning, you must note his use of capitalization. When the words "Holy Spirit" are capitalized in his books, he is talking about God and not what orthodoxy understands as the third Member of the Godhead, because he says there is no such person. When the words "holy spirit" are not capitalized, he refers to a gift that Christians receive from God. So *Holy Spirit is God* and *holy spirit is spiritual abilities*, particularly speaking in tongues. In Wierwille's theology, a Christian is not filled with the Holy Spirit, as Paul teaches in Ephesians 5:18, but he is filled with holy spirit.[2]

To Wierwille, then, the holy spirit is a spiritual ability—the power conferred at Pentecost—instead of a part of the Godhead: "The gift from the Holy Spirit, the Giver, is . . . holy spirit, power from on high, spiritual abilities, enablements. . . . The gift is holy spirit . . . which is an inherent spiritual ability. This gift is 'Christ in you, the hope of Glory' with all its fullness."[3] Thus, says Wierwille, when God the Father (the *H*oly *S*pirit) gives spiritual abilities, that is, *h*oly *s*pirit, that is

---

*Just as Wierwille's view of Christ is nothing more than a rerun of second- and third-century Monarchianism, likewise his view of the Holy Spirit is a rerun of *Macedonianism*. Macedonius (c.341) taught that the Holy Spirit was not a person but a divine energy throughout the universe. His heresy was condemned by the church at the First Council of Constantinople in A.D. 381.

"Christ in you, the hope of glory." That is the same as the human spirit and constitutes the divinity within man that was lost through the Fall.

You must further understand Wierwille's doctrine of man to begin to comprehend his doctrine of the Holy Spirit. He says that man was created by God as *body*, *soul*, and *spirit*—which is true. However, when Adam sinned, "The Spirit disappeared. The spirit was called dead in that it was no longer there. Their entire spiritual connection with God was lost. From that very day, Adam and Eve were just body and soul—as any other animal."[4] So, natural man in Wierwille's scheme of things is merely body and soul, just like all the rest of the animals. At the new birth, man receives the gift of holy spirit, or a spiritual nature.

However, according to the Bible, man is not a mere animal prior to his conversion. He still has a spirit, even though it is dead until regenerated by the Holy Spirit. But Wierwille disagrees with Scripture and says that man's spirit is nonexistent. Because Jesus was the "second Adam," reasons Wierwille, God created within Him a human spirit intact, and by its power Christ was able to live a life of sinless perfection. He was, therefore, exalted by God to a position from which He confers the "gift of the holy spirit" to those seeking salvation—and this is always evidenced by speaking in tongues. This human spirit, thus reinstated, is a force distinct from body and soul, unable to sin, and is the source of power for the "abundant living" The Way so loudly offers. This human spirit is now supposed to give the person supernatural, miraculous powers. God, says Wierwille, has thus shown us how to be little Jesuses ourselves.

However, there is not one Scripture verse to support this theory of "Holy Spirit" and "holy spirit." The Bible says, "There is . . . one Spirit, . . . one Lord, . . . one God and Father of all" (Ephesians 4:4-6). If the

Holy Spirit were the Father, it is unlikely that Scripture would continually make such a distinction between them. (See also Isaiah 48:16; 1 Corinthians 2:10-14; 2 Corinthians 13:14; Ephesians 4:30; 1 Peter 1:2).

John 15:26 says, "When the Helper comes, whom I will send to you from the Father, that is the Spirit of truth, who proceeds from the Father, He will bear witness of Me." If Mr. Wierwille is correct in his doctrine, then this passage is reduced to shambles and would have to read: "When the Father comes, whom I will send to you from the Father, that is the Father, who proceeds from the Father, He will bear witness of Me." That would be an obviously ludicrous rendering of this crucial passage; it would make the verse meaningless and contradictory.

SPEAKING IN TONGUES

Speaking in tongues is very crucial in Wierwille's theological scheme of things. He declares he can bring any Christian into the experience of speaking in tongues if that Christian so desires.[5] However, it was quite a struggle for him to manifest tongues the first time.

Wierwille has vividly recounted the frustrating search that, among other things, led him to study and memorize 385 Bible verses that refer to the Holy Spirit. Seeking more light on the subject of speaking in tongues, he questioned theologians and attended meetings of various groups. He was disturbed by emotional excesses he witnessed, yet longed for ability to speak in tongues himself.[6]

But then the turning point came. He received an invitation to attend a Full Gospel rally in Tulsa, Oklahoma. Oral Roberts was to be one of the key speakers. That was in the winter of 1951. In desperation, he decided to attend. After he arrived and checked in at his hotel, he met some other people who were there for the rally and told them of his need. A small group of "nine great men" met in one room to lay hands on him to receive the gift of tongues. In usual Pentecostal fashion they gathered around him and laid on hands. Several people began to speak unintelligibly. Then one of them told him to do the same.

A rather humorous bit of deception by Wierwille followed. In response to the request to speak in another language, he quoted the first chapter of John in Greek. The men, who did not know Greek, became excited, said he had "received," and urged that he speak in still another language. Wierwille did so. He quoted from Genesis in Hebrew. At the evening rally, one of the men announced that a Van Wert pastor had been led into tongues-speaking. But Wierwille was sick at heart, knowing he had not spoken in tongues.

Wierwille was also angry and confused; he decided to go home. But he got snowed in. Then through a series of other events, he met a man by the name of J. E. Stiles. Stiles went through some Scripture and began to work with Wierwille. After a time, Wierwille says, he experienced speaking a language he did not know. He says he spoke in tongues, prayed, and read the Bible all night. He was jubilant.[7]

From that time on, Wierwille began to incorporate this teaching and practice in his ministry. It now has become central in importance—so much so that he says speaking in tongues is the *only* real proof of the Holy Spirit. Consider the following statements:

> And you have no proof of God's resurrection 'till you speak in tongues.[8]

> The speaking in tongues was the external manifestation of the receiving of the gift of holy spirit.[9]

Speaking in tongues is central in all Way meetings and services. According to Wierwille, speaking in tongues is the only way truly to worship in the spirit. He says that to worship in the spirit, "We must operate a manifestation of the gift, holy spirit. The one manifestation of holy spirit which produces true worship is speaking in tongues."[10] Therefore, each Way meeting begins with the leader asking for several people to manifest tongues and interpret them. One woman who left The Way said that fact alone put such pressure on her at every meeting that she was nervous and insecure, always wondering if she would be the one called on at random to manifest tongues and interpret. This is one of the things that is taught toward the end of the initial PFAL course. Every Way believer is supposed to have received that manifestation and to practice it regularly.

Wierwille says that just as someone had to teach him, so "you could never speak in tongues if someone didn't teach. You gotta get it through teaching."[11] Now he says that he can teach any Christian who will obey him. In his little booklet *How to Speak in Tongues*, he gives the following instructions and explanations:

> Sit quietly and do exactly as I instruct. . . . In a moment I want you to open your mouth wide and breathe in. . . . Thank God for having filled you with the fullness of the power of His holy spirit. . . . When you begin to speak in tongues, move your lips, your throat, your tongue. Speak forth. When you have finished one word, speak another. Do not pay any attention to what you are thinking. . . . You are magnifying God no matter what the words sound like to your ears. . . . You are speaking in tongues.[12]

Both his teachings and his practices concerning speaking in tongues are very similar to much of what goes on today in Pentecostal and charismatic circles. This is understandable when we remember that those were the "groups" who "taught" him how to experience and manifest the gift. However, his interpretation would now greatly differ from their doctrine of the Holy Spirit.

The Bible does speak of a true gift of tongues. However, because of his faulty doctrine of the Holy Spirit, I would have to say that the tongues of The Way are false. Because they cannot be from the Holy Spirit of God, they must be either a psychic phenomenon or a satanically induced phenomenon. It must also be remembered that tongues are not an exclusively Christian practice. Satan is the master counterfeiter; speaking in tongues was practiced in pre-Christian times and in pagan religions.

So here is but another of the strands in Wierwille's theology. Holy Spirit (capital letters) is another name for God; but holy spirit (small letters) is spiritual abilities, particularly speaking in tongues.

9

Wierwille and the Word: The Bible

> You see, I've done one thing in my life. And this started in 1943, sir. I told God I'd do my utmost to rightly divide His Word, and, sir, that's what I've tried to do for 35 years.
>
> Victor Paul Wierwille[1]

If there is one thing Wierwille has convinced his followers of, it is that he is a Bible scholar and teacher. I once heard him tell a gathering of Way people: "It's a great privilege to hold forth the greatness of the Word all across the country! That's all I do is teach the Word, baby! . . . The Way ministry teaches nothing but the Word. . . . We research the Word of God and let the chips fall where they will!"[2]

He constantly says that "the Word of God is the will of God" and talks about his "working the Word" and "rightly dividing the Word." By a frequent use of the phrase "biblical research and teaching ministry," he and his followers imply that they have gone deeper into the Word and done a more thorough study than anyone else.

They often say that The Way is a "biblical research and teaching ministry" and not a "teaching and research ministry." In saying that, they are implying that they research first and then accurately teach the results; whereas others teach first and then as an afterthought do their research.

Wierwille would have us believe that he alone of all the Bible scholars in the world is rightly dividing and teaching the Word. In fact, he clearly says that when he recounts that God promised to teach him the Word of God as it had not been understood since the time of Christ, if he would but teach others.[3] In essence, he is claiming for himself what the apostle Paul claimed when he wrote: "For I would have you know, brethren, that the gospel which was preached by me is not according to man. For I neither received it from man, nor was I taught it, but I received it through a revelation of Jesus Christ" (Galatians 1:11-12).

You will often hear Way members say about Wierwille: "He is the greatest teacher since the time of the apostles because he teaches by revelation." Just as God gave Moses the Decalogue face to face and gave Paul direct revelation of the "mystery" of Christ (Romans 16:25; Ephesians 3:3), so Wierwille is saying that he now has received instruction on the Word as it has not been given since the first century. And he has revealed those keys for correctly understanding the Bible in his PFAL course. He assures his prospective student:

> The Bible is not difficult. . . . The reason this book is so difficult is because that's what we've been told it was! It isn't difficult. If you take our course we will give you all of the keys to God's Word so you can unlock it for yourself—so you can understand it.[4]

It must be pointed out, however, that the Bible is not an easy book to understand. The apostle Peter recognized this truth in reference to the writings of his fellow apostle Paul. He said there are many things in Paul's writings, as in other parts of Scripture, that are hard to understand; so the untaught and unstable twist and distort them, as they do the rest of Scripture (2 Peter 3:15-16). The Ethiopian eunuch realized that the Scriptures are not easy to understand when he was reading Isaiah. Philip ran beside his chariot and asked him if he understood what he was reading. "How could I," replied the eunuch, "unless someone guides me?" (Acts 8:31).

So, contrary to Wierwille's teaching, the Bible is not always an easy book to interpret. That is why the early believers were "devoting themselves to the apostles' teaching" (Acts 2:42). Wierwille would have his followers believe that he is the modern-day apostle who will give them truths that have been lost since those original apostles died.

His approach to establishing himself as a Bible scholar is fascinating. When I once heard him speak, he said this:

> The other night I was at Johns Hopkins University and there was a professor of Greek and Latin in the audience. He asked to meet me afterwards. When we met, you know what he said? He said, "Dr. Wierwille, I want to thank you for this service tonight. I've never sat in anything so electrifying! I never saw anybody use Greek as effectively as you did!"[5]

BIBLE SCHOLARSHIP OR BIBLE GIMMICKS?

As I said earlier in this book, Wierwille has a flair for theatrics and showmanship. Every act has got to have a gimmick, and Wierwille has his. He loves to use word games that make him look like a real researcher and scholar. These are his "warm-ups" on a crowd. Here is one of his favorites: he says that *four* were crucified with Christ instead of two. "You should have heard them crow,'' says Wierwille, ''the first time I came up with the four crucified with Jesus! Man, they were mad!''[6]

How did he arrive at that earthshaking and life-changing discovery? Well, Matthew says that there were ''two robbers'' who were crucified with Jesus (Matthew 27:38), and Luke says ''two . . . criminals'' (Luke 23:32). And anybody who can do simple math, reasons Wierwille, can see that two robbers plus two criminals equals four men. Further, says Wierwille, the victims died upon stakes instead of crosses. However, if he would read the entire four gospel accounts comparatively, he would see, as John clearly said, that Jesus was crucified between *two* men, ''one on either side, and Jesus in between'' (John 19:18). It does not say ''two on each side of Jesus.''

Another of his favorite lines is that Christ was crucified on Wednesday instead of Friday. This is a belief similar to the one held by Herbert W. Armstrong and his ''World Wide Church of God'' cult. ''Jesus Christ cannot have died on Friday and gotten up on Easter Sunday,'' Wierwille has said. ''Start with first things, son. Do your math. Two plus two. Then when you want to go to calculus, we'll run.''[7] But there are also many orthodox Christians who do not believe that Jesus died on Good Friday. Those who hold to a literal seventy-two-hour period of time say that he had to have been crucified on Wednesday. That would have to be so because of Christ's association with the prophet Jonah, who was in the belly of the fish for ''three days and three nights'' (Matthew 12:40). Those who hold to Good Friday are divided into two groups. There are those who say that the ''three days and three nights'' is a Hebrew idiom in which any part of the day is symbolic of a complete ''day and night.'' Jesus therefore was dead for parts of three days: Friday, Saturday, and Sunday. In Hebrew idiom that would equal three full days and nights. Those who hold to Friday literally rather than as a Hebrew idiom say that Christ was in the grave only two nights.

But the point is this: the day Christ died should be no subject of division among true Christians. That He did die and was resurrected is the central issue that all Christians agree upon. To try to make an issue out of Wednesday as the day of the crucifixion is neither new nor of prime importance. Wierwille's doing so only reveals his true purpose—to try to set himself up as an accurate researcher of the Word who has discovered truths that have been missed for nineteen hundred years. You can be assured that Wierwille will never make any new discoveries or raise any new issues that other Bible scholars have not long known about.

The purpose, then, of Wierwille's majoring on such minor points is to suggest to his hearers and readers that the church has deceived them all these years. After all, if the church cannot even add two plus two when it comes to the Word, it is not nearly ready to handle the real "calculus" of the Word! If it has misled you on the number of thieves crucified with Christ—and the day on which He was crucified—in how many more places have you not been told the truth? Do you see his ploy?

THE BIBLICAL ORIGINALS: GREEK OR ARAMAIC?

As I have said, Wierwille wants people to believe that he is a great Bible researcher and scholar. He and his followers make a big issue of the *Peshitta* and other Eastern texts that they say are the only truly reliable ones. One of his understudies and "researchers," Walter Cummins, said: "Even the most objective critics of the New Testament have concluded that a formal Aramaic document lies behind the Greek text of the New Testament."[8] You will constantly hear Wierwille and other Way teachers referring to Aramaic and seeking to defend their various unique biblical interpretations by such references. The following statement by Wierwille is typical:

> I'm speaking in Estrengeelo Aramaic. I'm not
> speaking Greek. Estrengeelo preceded Greek.
> Greek is a translation, 'cause this is the position of
> The Way ministry . . . that the originals were all
> written in Estrengeelo Aramaic. And that Greek
> was a translation off of those. . . . Paul did not
> write in Greek.[9]

So Paul and the other disciples, says Wierwille, did not write in Greek but in Aramaic. Why then is this not taught in other seminaries and Bible centers around the world? "Because you've lied about Greek being the original so long you gotta keep lying 'cause you got all your Greek chairs endowed," says Wierwille.[10] So money is the issue, not true scholarship, says Wierwille.

The Way teaches that the people of the New Testament were all Aramaic-speaking people who were out of touch with the Greek world or disliked its language and culture. Aramaic was the language of the East and Greek was the language of the West. But The Way says that even though the New Testament writers originally wrote in Aramaic, they soon made translations into Greek for the benefit of the Greek-speaking culture in the West. That is when the corruption of the original Aramaic texts supposedly occurred. When the original texts were translated into Greek, it is claimed, words had to be invented to convey properly the meaning of the inspired Aramaic—hence the evidence of Aramaic words in our Greek text today.

Remember our talking about the Council of Nicaea of A.D. 325? You will recall that Wierwille said it was pro-West and anti-East. Because the West was Greek-speaking and the East Aramaic-speaking, and because Nicaea was Occidental (Western)-dominated, herefore, says The Way, the Eastern text has not been well known in the West.[11]

Here is The Way's "scholarly" conclusion on the matter:

> Because of the practical and doctrinal error that followed the original work of the apostles from the end of the first century on, words were changed, added and omitted in the Aramaic and the Greek texts. At times certain people even left out whole books from the New Testament because it disagreed with what they believed. Nevertheless, the New Testament as we have it today stems from an Aramaic original and various translations in Greek, Latin, Coptic and other languages.[12]

Does Bible Scholarship Agree?

I have checked with various professors of Greek about this matter of the original New Testament's being written in Aramaic, and their response to the matter was unanimous: No reputable Bible scholar in the world believes what Wierwille is teaching. "Without any shadow of a doubt," said one professor, "the originals were in Greek and not Aramaic."

In an essay entitled "The Languages Spoken by Jesus," Philip Hughes, professor at Westminster Theological Seminary, says:

> It is well established that Greek was the *lingua franca* of the Mediterranean world in the apostolic period. . . . If, as the evidence indicates, the purpose of the Church was missionary from the outset . . . with the aim of proclaiming the gospel to all men everywhere in the world, then when the time came for committing anything to writing, the only reasonable course to take was to write the message in the *lingua franca* of the known world, *koine* Greek.[13]

That is certainly not to say that Aramaic was not used. "Aramaic was no doubt the spoken language of the Lord and His disciples."[14] It had been the "*lingua franca* of the Near East in the sixth through fourth centuries B.C., until the conquest of Alexander the Great."[15] Because of that, there have been those—notably C.C. Torrey, to whom Wierwille and other Way teachers often refer—who said that the originals were Aramaic instead of Greek. However, one no less than W. F. Albright, the world's foremost biblical archaeologist until his death, did not agree. He said, "There is absolutely no trace so far of a continuous Aramaic literary tradition."[16]

So, biblical research just does not confirm the theory of Aramaic originals. Since the *lingua franca*, or common language, of the then-known world was Greek and not Aramaic, the only way the Great Commission of Christ would be fulfilled was for the disciples to use Greek as their medium of written communication.

Not only do scholars not agree with Wierwille's Aramaic originals concept, but they also do not agree with his overall use of Greek. As Dr. Walter Martin, foremost cult authority in America, said to me concerning Wierwille's so-called scholarship, "His interpretations just won't stand up under accurate Greek scholarship. There is not a competent New Testament Greek scholar today who supports his interpretation. He is just dishonest to the biblical languages."

CONCLUSIONS

Wierwille is not the accurate Bible scholar and researcher he professes to be. He certainly is *not* "rightly dividing the Word." However, he *is* "working it" and in the process making it say what it does not say. He ends up in bibliolatry, or worship of the Word, rather than worship of its main revelation, the God-man, Jesus Christ. Wierwille is therefore guilty of twisting the Word to his own destruction (2 Peter 3:16).

10

Strange Doctrines: Other Way Teachings

Paul admonished Timothy to remain in Ephesus "in order that you may instruct certain men not to teach strange doctrines" (1 Timothy 1:3). Thus far we have covered the main points of Wierwille's "different gospel." There are many more, the adequate treatment of which would take several more books. Therefore, having dealt with the major heresies concerning the Trinity and the deity of Christ, I shall only list some of Wierwille's other "strange doctrines." This is just so that you will not get caught off guard if you are ever confronted with them by some Way member.

1. Wierwille teaches that Christ's cry from the cross: "*Eli, Eli, lama sabachthani?*," or "My God, My God, Why hast Thou forsaken Me?," was not a cry of despair but of triumph. From his Aramaic "research" he interprets the cry this way: "My God, my God, for this purpose was I spared, for this purpose was I kept, for this purpose came I into the world, for this purpose was I reserved." He says that "My God, my God, why hast Thou forsaken Me?" is the Occidental translation and is erroneous.[1]

97

The familiar words that Jesus was quoting from the cross were from Psalm 22:1. On the cross, the perfect Man, Jesus, "who knew no sin," was being made "to be sin on our behalf, that we might become the righteousness of God in Him" (2 Corinthians 5:21). It was during those three hours of supernatural darkness between noon and three o'clock that God "caused the iniquity of us all to fall on Him" (Isaiah 53:6). It was then that Jesus experienced and suffered on our behalf all the horror of separation from God that sin brings.

In reality, then, Christ's lament was a cry of despair for Him that ultimately means victory and triumph for the believer.

2. Like the Jehovah's Witnesses and Armstrong, Wierwille teaches that human beings do not have immortal souls. They remain dead upon physical death until the final resurrection. He teaches that "when you are dead, you are dead and there is none in Heaven now but Jesus." This is, of course, the familiar doctrine known as "soul sleep." According to Wierwille, the Christian upon death does not go to be with Christ but remains unconscious until the resurrection.[2]

Contrary to this, the apostle Paul clearly says, "We . . . prefer rather to be absent from the body and to be at home with the Lord" (2 Corinthians 5:8). Paul also spoke of his "desire to depart [this life through death] and be with Christ" (Philippians 1:23). Moses and Elijah were clearly not dead or in some state of "soul sleep," for they appeared with Christ on the mount of transfiguration (Matthew 17:3; Mark 9:4). In Jesus' story of the rich man and Lazarus, there was no soul sleep. Both men were in a conscious state after death, Lazarus in Abraham's bosom and the rich man in torment (Luke 16:19-31). Also, Jesus said to the penitent thief on the cross, "Truly I say to you, today you shall be with Me in Paradise" (Luke 23:43).

So the doctrine of "soul sleep" is just not biblical, and in teaching it Wierwille has aligned himself with the cults of the Jehovah's Witnesses and Armstrongism.

3. Another of Wierwille's strange doctrines is that water baptism is not for Christians. He says that it was instituted by God for Israel only, and then only for a limited time. Today, he says, we are under grace and free from bondage to the Law and its practices. The key text that Wierwille tries to use to substantiate his doctrine is Acts 1:5: "For John baptized with water, but you shall be baptized with the Holy Spirit not many days from now." The only baptism for Christians, then, says Wierwille, is the baptism of holy spirit. (There are the little "h" and "s" again. Remember that according to Wierwille, the Holy Spirit is not a person.) He stresses that because water baptism is not mentioned in Acts 2,8,9, and 19, nor in Romans, 1 or 2 Corinthians, Galatians, Ephesians, Philippians, Colossians, or Thessalonians, it is not important. Wierwille also denies that Matthew 28:19, with its command of baptism, was ever carried out by the disciples. Furthermore, he says, the phrase "in the name of the Father and the Son and the Holy Spirit" was not in the *original* Aramaic Word of God. As usual, he cites no documentation for that statement.

Wierwille concedes that Matthew 28:19 appears in all extant manuscripts (the oldest date from the fourth century when, he says, the doctrine of the Trinity was evolving). He suggests that scribes could easily have inserted "in the name of the Father, and of the Son, and of the Holy Ghost." Wierwille concludes, "This must have been what happened."[3]

Again, note his anti trinitarian presupposition. So it was those pro trinitarian Nicene theologians who probably are to blame for the phrase! Also, notice the use of the subjunctive: "This *must* have been what happened" (emphasis added). His bias is obvious.

In fact, every extant ancient manuscript and every valid translation of the Bible proves Matthew 28:19 to be completely valid. The phrase "in the name of the Father and of the Son and of the Holy Spirit" was necessary to distinguish this new Christian sacrament from Jewish baptism or the baptism of John the Baptist. Also, every reference to baptism from Acts on *cannot* be equated with spirit baptism, as Wierwille would have us believe. Consider the following verses:

> Acts 2:41: the three thousand who were baptized on the day of Pentecost
>
> Acts 8:12-16: those who were baptized during the Samaritan revival
>
> Acts 8:38: the baptism of the Ethiopian eunuch by Philip
>
> Acts 9:18: the baptism of Paul after his conversion (cf. Acts 22:16)
>
> Acts 10:47-48: the baptism of Cornelius and his household
>
> Acts 16:15: the baptism of Lydia and her household
>
> Acts 16:33: the baptism of the Philippian jailer and his household
>
> Acts 18:8: the baptism of the Corinthians
>
> Acts 19:3-5: the baptism of John's disciples at Ephesus
>
> 1 Corinthians 1:13-16: the baptism of certain persons by Paul

So, contrary to what Wierwille teaches, water baptism is clearly biblical and has been the practice of all orthodox Christians for over nineteen hundred years, in obedience to the command of Christ.

SUMMARY

There are other novel teachings that I will not take space to cover, such as the idea that Christians are supposed never to get sick. Christ conquered all sickness, teaches Wierwille, and all we have to do is rebuke it.* So sickness can *never* be an instrument of the Lord for our good; according to Wierwille, sickness is never the will of God. He has even been quietly teaching of late that we can control our dying!

The Way also de-emphasizes Christmas and Easter as secondary but celebrates Pentecost, which Wierwille considers the most important of Christian holy days.

My own summary of Wierwille's "strange doctrines" is what Paul warned young Timothy about:

> The time will come when they will not endure sound doctrine; but wanting to have their ears tickled, they will accumulate for themselves teachers in accordance to their own desires; and will turn away their ears from the truth, and will turn aside to myths [2 Timothy 4:3-4].

---

*The most widely publicized incident highlighting Wierwille's teaching on sickness and healing concerns Timothy Goodwin. He is a twenty-five-year-old quadriplegic who was left in that condition after an automobile accident on a Los Angeles freeway. Goodwin says that The Way assured him that he would be healed within one year of giving them 15 percent of his $1.4 million insurance settlement check. That came to $210,000. The check was written out by Wierwille and signed by Goodwin with a pen held between his teeth. Checks for a Cadillac and a BMW automobile for the Wierwilles were similarly signed. When months passed and there was no healing, Goodwin filed a $300,000 lawsuit against Wierwille and his brother Harry, who was until his death the secretary-treasurer of The Way. Goodwin also charged them with mental and physical abuse. The Wierwilles responded with a countersuit of $850,000 against Goodwin. They said that he was harassing them with adverse publicity. The case was settled out of court, with the Wierwilles repaying Goodwin in full.

11

The Way: A Dead End

The doctrinal errors that we have been discussing are only part of the unbiblical interpretations to be found in Mr. Wierwille's writings. Without doubt, he is a false prophet deceiving many—he, himself, apparently being the most deceived of all. As Paul said, when man refuses to "receive the love of the truth so as to be saved. . . . God will send upon them a deluding influence so that they might believe what is false" (2 Thessalonians 2:10-11). Mr. Wierwille is certainly in that category.

Two Kinds of False Prophets

In studying The Way and many other cults, I have come to realize there are two kinds of false prophets. First, there are the professional religious swindlers and cheats who deliberately deceive people for personal gain. Many people like that may have had at one time a legitimate calling from God upon their lives. However, that call has been perverted and abused through greed and pride. Many start out through the power of love but end in the love of power.

103

Second, there are those who are sincere in their zeal and dedication. They really have come to believe that their delusions are God's truth for man. Most of them claim to have received a "divine visitation" that has given them some new and special "light," or "revelation." They soon are zealously propagating it as God's latest truth to the world. They are for the most part absolutely sincere, but nevertheless self-deluded, individuals. Some are suffering under a "messianic" or "prophetic" complex concerning their supposed revelation and commission from God. Mr. Wierwille is probably in this second category. In listening to him speak, I was struck with his apparent sincerity and his burning conviction that he really does have God's truth for people today.

So, there are two kinds of false prophets: the ones who are false and know it and the ones who are false and do not know it. However, either kind of false prophet will lead individuals to spiritual destruction, even though one is knowingly doing it and the other is unknowingly doing it.

WIERWILLE'S DETOUR FROM THE WAY

Mr. Wierwille has had both a Christian background and a thorough exposure to sound biblical teaching. Tragically, he has chosen to reject them. Perhaps it was the dead orthodoxy of his own church background that caused him to do this. This cannot be said for sure, but I got that idea from some of his negative statements about the church he grew up in when I heard him speak. In seeking and sifting for truth, we are all prone to "throw out the baby" with the proverbial bathwater. In essence, that is exactly what Wierwille did. In throwing out some of the polluted ecclesiastical bathwater of his church experience and theological education, he also threw out the divinely incarnate Babe of Bethlehem. But from his study of church history, he should have known better. If he were truly the Bible scholar he claims to be, he would surely have seen the errors of his thinking and realized his repetition of second- and third-century heresies that had all been condemned by the church councils. Therefore, I believe that the inspired words of the apostle Paul concerning those who reject God's truth definitely apply to Mr. Wierwille and many of his followers:

> They are without excuse. For even though they knew God, they did not honor Him as God. . . . they became futile in their speculations, and their foolish heart was darkened. Professing to be wise ["30 years of biblical study and research"], they became fools. . . . they exchanged the truth of God [that He is triune in nature] for a lie [*Jesus Christ Is Not God*], and worshiped and served the creature [If Jesus Christ is not God, He is nothing more than a deified creature] rather than the Creator [Romans 1:20-22, 25].

What the apostle John said of the false teachers and prophets of his day must, tragically, also be said of Mr. Wierwille:

> They went out from us [Wierwille left the Christian ministry], but they were not really of us. . . . Who is the liar but the one who denies that Jesus is the Christ [which Wierwille's book *Jesus Christ Is Not God* does]? This is the antichrist, the one who denies the Father and the Son. Whoever denies the Son does not have the Father [1 John 2:19, 22-23; cf. Matthew 24:24; John 14:7; 1 Corinthians 11:19; 2 Corinthians 11:13; 1 Thessalonians 5:21; 2 Timothy 2:19].

CONDEMNED BY HIS WORDS

According to the Bible, then, Wierwille is of the antichrist and teaches a ''different gospel'' about ''another

Jesus" that is inspired by a "different spirit" (2 Corinthians 11:4; Galatians 1:6-8; 1 John 2:22). One day he will have to answer for his words, which of themselves will condemn him. As Jesus said: "And I say to you, that every careless word that men shall speak, they shall render account for it in the day of judgment. For by your words you shall be justified, and by your words you shall be condemned" (Matthew 12:36-37). Some of the very words and statments that will judge Wierwille on that day are the following:

> Why don't we look for a way to build the Word rather than tear it to pieces?[1]
>
> Every influence which is not based upon the accuracy of God's Word shall come to naught.[2]
>
> We ought to think it supremely important to accurately divide that Word.[3]
>
> If my research is a wrong-dividing of God's Word, then I stand before God as an unapproved workman. Either way I accept full responsibility.[4]

If Mr. Wierwille had heeded the biblical warning "that no prophecy of Scripture is a matter of one's own interpretation" (2 Peter 1:20), he might not have become so sincerely self-deceived. Any time one person sets up himself as the undisputed leader, chief theologian, exegete of Scripture, and official voice of God, he is headed for self-deception and error. That is why the Bible says, "In *abundance* of counselors there is victory" (Proverbs 11:14, emphasis added). That is also at least one of the reasons why Christ made us part of a diverse body of believers, with the many gifts of His Holy Spirit to serve as checks and balances against this kind of biblical and spiritual individualism. We can only hope and pray that Mr. Wierwille will humble himself and submit his "interpretations'' and ''biblical research'' to the scrutiny and correction of the many true earlier and contemporary scholars who radically disagree with his so-called research, scholarship, and biblical exegesis.

So I state, in agreement with both Scripture and Christian history, that the Word according to Wierwille was not known in the first century and is finding wide acceptance today only because of biblical and historical ignorance on the part of its adherents.

> There is a way which seems right to a man, but its end is the way of death [Proverbs 14:12].

> Enter by the narrow gate; for the gate is wide, and the way is broad that leads to destruction, and many are those who enter by it. For the gate is small, and the way is narrow that leads to life, and few are those who find it [Matthew 7: 13-14].

12

Lost Along the Way: Are Members of The Way Unsaved?

As we approach the end of this study, I would like to pose a question that I am sure you have been asking yourself: Are there Christians in The Way, or are all of the Way people lost? That is certainly a question I have found myself grappling with in preparing this book. Of course, in the final analysis, God is the only one capable of answering the question. However, I think that there are a number of young people in The Way who are Christians. I talked to Dr. Walter Martin about this; he expressed his belief this way: "There are many good Christian kids who are turned off to the church but are still looking for spiritual reality. Many of them have gotten sucked in by Wierwille and The Way."

My interviews over the past several years with both current and former Way members have confirmed that opinion. I have talked to a number of young Christians who have been drawn into The Way through their spiritual naiveté. My experience confirms that it is young Christians and nominal Christians who are disillusioned with the institutional church that are particularly vulnerable to The Way.

Even though there are Christians in The Way, they cannot hope to continue their involvement—accepting all of its beliefs and doctrines—and still remain healthy, maturing Christians. *They will eventually have to go one way or the other.* Either they will walk further into the shadows and darkness of Mr. Wierwille's delusion, or they will walk into the full, glorious, and liberating light of the gospel. Their faith must be purified and purged of "Wierwilleism" before the strong delusion that he apparently is under totally smothers their spiritual life as well. That is why every Christian must do all he can to "convince some, who doubt; save some, by snatching them out of the fire" (Jude 22-23, RSV) and bring them back into a "purity of devotion to Christ" (2 Corinthians 11:3).

We can only hope and pray that with Mr. Wierwille's emphasis on the Word, many of those young people will get past his novel interpretations, his Greek and Aramaic "exegesis," and his many personal trappings and subtle colorings to the pure Word of God. And from there may they establish a right knowledge of and saving relationship with the holy Son of God.

One young Christian couple I talked to were extricated that way. They had been new Christians and were invited to a twig meeting at the University of North Carolina. They were looking for fellowship, so they went, thinking that The Way was a good Christian organization that could teach them the Bible. Very quickly they were attracted by the love that was expressed toward them by the twig leaders. Soon pressure was applied to take the PFAL course; they were promised that they would get all their Bible questions answered there. After a struggle over the decision about the two hundred dollars it was going to cost them, they finally signed up and began the course.

About that time they received a warning from the man who had led them to the Lord. He had read my earlier booklet on The Way and had even sent them a copy. However, inasmuch as they had already paid for the PFAL course (there are no refunds), they decided to go ahead and take it. But each evening before going they prayed that the Holy Spirit would show them any questionable areas in Wierwille's teaching.

"We were new Christians and were not knowledgeable about the Bible and basic Christian doctrines," the wife told me. "But we prayed that the Holy Spirit would give us conflict," said the husband, "that He would somehow reveal to us what was wrong. And it was amazing how God did it!" Even though they completed the course, their comment was, "The more we took it, the more questions and conflicts we had—especially when Wierwille started on his interpretation of John 1!"

Jesus said that one of the ministries of His Holy Spirit is to "guide you into all the truth" (John 16:13). He certainly did so with the couple I just mentioned. However, this ministry will be difficult for Him to perform in the lives of those caught in the delusion of The Way in the sense that, because Mr. Wierwille has denied the Trinity, they are not seeking or very receptive to His leading. Wierwille has reduced the person of the Holy Spirit to an impersonal force. He has replaced the vital guiding and instructing ministry of the Holy Spirit with his own PFAL course, in which *he* gives his followers all of the "keys" to correct biblical interpretation and understanding.

So Christians must pray that God will, through the power of His Word and the ministry of His Holy Spirit, lead those within the organization who are sincerely seeking truth into its fullness, which would mean that they would come into a pure understanding of and relationship with the One who said of Himself, "I am . . . the truth" (John 14:6).

I still trust that as many Way followers read and study

God's Word—which is "living and active and sharper than any two-edged sword" (Hebrews 4:12)—the Holy Spirit will help them "handl[e] accurately the word of truth" (2 Timothy 2:15). Then God's Word, accurately understood, will separate for them the delusions of Mr. Wierwille from the revelation of the biblical writers concerning the deity of Jesus Christ. Thereby they might be saved.

That is exactly what happened to a friend of mine. Let him tell you his story. It is a classic study in how someone gets caught up in a cult like The Way:

> I became acquainted with The Way International and the teachings of Victor Paul Wierwille while at North Carolina State University working on a Ph.D. in plant pathology. A fellow graduate student invited me to a meeting where "The Doctor" was to speak. Expecting only to hear God's Word taught, I was not prepared to meet a wolf in sheep's clothing. Since I was equipped with little more than a "born-again experience" dating back nineteen years, my ignorance of Bible truths made me a prime candidate for cultic involvement. My innocence was mostly self-imposed, for there had been ample opportunities to become rooted in correct doctrine.
>
> I was reared by loving Christian parents. I was saved at nine and I was active in my Southern Baptist church. I began to teach Sunday school at 17. My father was a deacon and my older brother a well educated Baptist pastor. I graduated from a church-affiliated university having had courses in both Old and New Testament. I married a lovely Christian girl from strong Methodist stock.
>
> From high school on, academic achievements, earning money, and recreation largely had replaced

a walk with Jesus as my goals. When around church people, my scant Bible study was effectively masked by a willingness to talk at length on what little I did know. There were many occasions when I sensed that the Lord had plans for me if I would only cooperate; but I did not. . . .

I made it through most of my college career on ability, perseverance, and the prayerful support of others. It was sometimes gratifying, but often a lonely trek. I knew in my heart that somewhere, somehow there was a step up to a closer walk with God, but I wanted it to be dramatic, exciting, and without going cold-turkey from the world.

In the twisted doctrines of The Way I found the gimmicks I was looking for. They said all the denominational churches were largely wrong and the real abundant life was in "The Word" as rightly divided by the apostle for this age, Victor Paul Wierwille, and the semi-communal way of life his proselytes had adopted.

Once on the inside, I readily accepted that you must speak in tongues to truly worship God and otherwise operate the manifestations of the Holy Spirit as taught by Wierwille in his classes on "Power for Abundant Living" (PFAL). The fact that Jesus had already baptized me with the Holy Spirit seemed to be played down in lieu of the PFAL method.

Increasingly I began to realize that to be fully prepared to minister under the auspices of The Way would require a considerable outlay of money over a period of time. Many classes, seminars, books, and in-service training must be completed, each with a price tag.

Despite words of caution from both my wife and my pastor, I became turned on to this group and their apparent command of spiritual keys to the Kingdom. Soon after plunging headlong into The Way doctrines I met the kicker—''Jesus Christ is not God!'' The other teachings went down easily. That my Jesus was not part of the Trinity went down with great difficulty, as I forced myself to swallow it. I was spiritually ill and very confused. I wanted to fit in with The Way, but a diet of the Word diluted with a great deal of the world wasn't hitting the spot. So, I stopped going to ''twig,'' the indoctrination tool which was encouraged nightly. Guilt and countless doubts flooded my thoughts. Somehow, the Lord finally prepared my mind and heart for some straight doctrine. It came unannounced via a fellow from my Baptist Sunday school class, Don Jones. It seems he had a tape by someone named J. L. Williams on cults, and just thought I might like to hear it.

When I first heard The Way listed as a counter-Christian cult, I revolted at such heresy. But, I listened again and again until the proof was undeniable. Why, I had been taken! But, what will my old church friends say if I 'fess up? Boy! The pastor must be really disappointed! Where do I find the whole, unadultered truth? More questions, but this time with Jesus back beside me, once again I acknowledged Him as my Lord and my God. The prayer dam burst and I was flooded with the peace of God Himself. Now I would do as He willed for me, I promised.

Two days later, a door opened and I took my first steps to obey His call to magnify Jesus' name. I was to humbly but boldly go and expose Satan's presence in the midst of "religion." "Make my people aware of the cults—but let the world know that I AM is alive and well."

Thank you, Jesus! Thank you Don and J. L.! Thank you, Mary Lu, dearest wife ever! Thank you, Church, for praying for me; I'll see you all one day.

David A. Rickard [name changed]
January 13, 1977

Not only is David's story a classic example of how someone gets involved in a cult like The Way, but it is also a thrilling example of the corporate power of prayer and the witness of God's people. He was reared in the true way, took a detour into the wrong way, and finally returned to Christ, the Way, the Truth, and the Life. Every Christian should pray that David's story of restoration to the true way will be multiplied many times by other young Christians who have taken a similar detour.

A HAPPY ENDING

Every story needs a happy ending. Not all stories end happily: many of them are tragedies, especially when it comes to cultic involvement. Guyana will forever remind us of that. However, I want to close this book with a happy ending. Do you remember the letter at the beginning of the book? The one from the girl Sue in St. Louis, Missouri? The one who had become disillusioned with her church and was about to get caught up in The Way? After writing her and sending her my tape on The Way, I received this letter:

Dear J. L.,

I just wanted to write and thank you for writing such a nice letter.

I have listened to your tape and read your book, and in my heart I knew the things you were saying were true. But I found myself also getting angry about some things and feeling very defensive on The Way's behalf. I don't feel that way now.

As I told you in my first letter, I was seeking a church and also recovering from a broken relationship . . . I went through a year of deep depression . . . So when I met Ron from The Way, I not only admired his zeal for the Lord and his knowledge, I was very attracted to him. The battle I fought in my heart and mind was the worst battle I have ever had with the enemy!

Now the Lord has given me the victory! Your tape and book have really helped me tremendously. I deeply appreciated your personal letter which convinced me even further in my stand.

I am still seeking a purpose for my life and still searching for a new church, but I know "The Way" isn't the answer!

I will be praying for your ministry . . .

Jesus is Victor!

Love,

Sue

It is for all the Sues and Davids and others like them that I have written this book!

13

Postscript:
Marks of the Cults

One of the signs of the end times about which Christ warned His followers was an increase of false Christs, prophets, and teachers (Matthew 24:11). He said many of these would show great signs and wonders and deceive, if possible, even the elect (Matthew 24:24). The apostle Paul warned that the devil disguises himself as an "angel of light" (2 Corinthians 11:14) in order to masquerade as Christ, who said that He is "the light of the world" (John 8:12). As such, Satan is the master of deceit. Many counterfeit faiths are on the market today. The Way is just one of an increasing number of these cults.

THE UNPAID BILLS OF THE CHURCH

We who are members of the church of Jesus Christ must face up to the fact that the success of these many cults is due in part to our failure. Many of the cultic criticisms of the church are well founded. Tragically, there is far too much cold, dead orthodoxy in the institutional church. Many churches do lack power, purpose,

117

and zeal. Many Christians' lives are listless. The late Dr. E. Stanley Jones described this kind of church: "They are faultily faultless, icily regular—and splendidly dull!" There is great truth then in what Dr. Van Baalen said in his book *Chaos of the Cults*: "The cults are the unpaid bills of the church." So if for no other reason, I believe God is allowing cults like The Way to arise and challenge our dead orthodoxy, lifeless rituals, theological emptiness, and lack of Bible study.

We cannot hope either to evangelize the lost or to prevail against the enemy with a casual "business as usual" spiritual attitude. We must realize we are involved in a struggle "against the rulers, against the powers, against the world forces of this darkness, against the spiritual forces of wickedness in the heavenly places" (Ephesians 6:12). Every Christian, therefore, needs to be totally equipped with the whole armor of God (Ephesians 6:10-17), and through prayer and supplication keep alert to the end with all perseverance (Ephesians 6:18).

Once we know the disguises of Satan, we shall be able readily to recognize any of his cultic counterfeits. The points below are general marks of cultic groups.[1] When you notice a group exemplifying these marks, be on guard, for you will know you are up against the devil, the adversary of your soul (1 Peter 5:8).

IDENTIFYING MARKS OF THE CULTS

1. **They all deviate from the Scriptures as God's total, complete, and final written revelation to man.** They usually have some "further" revelation that goes beyond what is revealed in the Bible. If they do use the Bible, they usually have their own "translations" or "interpretations." These are not generally true to the original biblical languages.

2. Because they deviate from the written Word (Bible),

they do not accept the living Word (Jesus) as the completely unique Son of God. Jesus may be very important in their theology, but not as God the Son, the second member of the Godhead. So they believe in and preach what Paul called "another Jesus."

3. **Most cults are also usually anti trinitarian.** They therefore do not accept the Holy Spirit as a coequal member of the triune Godhead. The Holy Spirit is not considered an actual person, but an "it" or a "divine influence."

4. **All cults have some extrabiblical figurehead that they follow.** He is their messiah or Christ-substitute. There is a blind allegiance to this person and the followers gather about this leader's interpretation of the Bible or world affairs or both. Some characteristics common to these cultic leaders are:

   a. *He is egocentric instead of Christocentric.* He promotes himself—God and Christ are secondary.
   b. *He lives under a delusion of grandeur,* this often verging on megalomania. He is always "first," "best," "the greatest in his field."
   c. *He often has delusions of persecution.* When his grandiose plans fail, he is never at fault or personally responsible. Someone else is always to blame.
   d. *He often has a "god complex."* He is his own authority. He claims that he hears the voice of God. Often he uses the phrase "God told me." In reality, he places himself beyond reason and Scripture.
   e. *He generally surrounds himself with inferior persons.* They ultimately become his "yes men." In doing so, they lose their identity in him

and become submissive defendants of his decisions.

f. *He often projects and supports a credible cause:* feeding the hungry, clothing the naked, helping young people on drugs, and so on.

g. *He habitually engages in the sensational.* He claims God's power to perform signs, wonders, and miracles. There is often emphasis on healing and other spectacular spiritual gifts. He often preys upon the wealthy, the physically ill, the emotionally starved, and people low on the socioeconomic scale.

h. *He always engages in great schemes for fundraising.* These are usually tax deductible. This money is often beyond the scrutiny of anyone but himself. There is often a personal amassing of wealth and a lavish life-style.

i. *He discredits the institutional church and minimizes its influence.* He constantly points out its weaknesses. He seeks to elevate his own position and power by contrast.

j. *He is subject to quick and drastic changes in behavior and action.* This is done without regard to principle, the teaching of Scripture, or responsibility to his supporters.

k. *He often attempts and accomplishes great things.* But in doing so he usually produces great havoc and division in the church.

l. *Usually he has a charismatic personality* with an ability to influence people—especially with regard to finances.

5. In spite of their radical deviation from or redefinition of biblical Christianity, **many cultic groups still insist they are fully entitled to be called "Christians."** They often believe they are the only true Christians left.

6. **They are for the most part earnest and sincere people who believe in what they profess.** Many of them have a "martyr complex" and see themselves as "God's remnant people." They are God's "persecuted saints," and they view all who oppose them as enemies of God.

7. **Many cultic groups are characterized by an end-of-the-world or last-days preoccupation.** There is often a great emphasis on prophecy and an overall apocalyptic aura.

8. **There is often a strong separation from the world's mentality.** It is evil and under the judgment of God. Many as a result adopt a communal or semicommunal life-style.

9. **They are autosoteric.** That is, they practice some form of self-salvation. Having rejected the justification accomplished by Christ, they seek to justify themselves by various kinds of works. This accounts for much of their zeal and dedication.

10. **Many cultic groups are characterized by an emphasis on self-sacrifice.** They are "high demand groups" that require a totalistic life-style.

11. **Most cultic groups vigorously oppose the institutional church.** They claim themselves to be the one true church.

12. **Most cultic groups are syncretistic by nature.** They are "religious eclectics" who have built their beliefs by picking and choosing from many sources. Their doctrine is usually a theological patchwork.

Not all cults will exemplify all of these marks. Some groups will be characterized by more of these marks than others. But when you see *any* of these marks being manifested, the spiritual caution light should go on.

As Christians, we do not seek to be exclusive or

legalistic. However, we must never compromise the biblical message of Christ, who said of Himself: "I am the way, and the truth, and the life; no one comes to the Father, but through Me" (John 14:6). He claimed to be the *full* and *final* revelation of God to man; the New Testament writers also attributed this uniqueness to Him: "And there is salvation in no one else; for there is no other name under heaven that has been given among men, by which we must be saved" (Acts 4:12).

Therefore, whether or not we or anyone else likes it, that leaves out Buddha, Muhammad, Confucius, Krishna, Maharji Ji, Bahaullah, Malcolm X, Mary Baker Eddy, Joseph Smith and Brigham Young, Charles and Myrtle Fillmore, Elijah Mohammed, Herbert W. and Garner Ted Armstrong, the Reverend Sun Myung Moon, and Victor Paul Wierwille. Of Christ alone it is said, "It was the Father's good pleasure for all the fulness to dwell in Him" (Colossians 1:19).

Remember, "A wolf does not become a sheep simply by wearing wool!"

Appendix 1:

Apologetic for the Deity of Christ

I would now like to accept a challenge made by Mr. Wierwille in the September 6, 1971, issue of *Time* Magazine. On page 54 of that issue he challenged: "You show me one place in the Bible where it says He (Jesus) is God . . . I don't want your rapping, your doubletalk, your triple talk: all I want is Scripture."

Since Mr. Wierwille asked for scriptural proof for the divinity of Christ, here it is. I shall quote only one scripture reference and cite others for the sake of space. I hope you will look up and mark these references in your own Bible. Also, the various points will only be stated, not amplified and interpreted as could be done if space permitted.

A SCRIPTURAL APOLOGETIC FOR THE DIVINITY OF CHRIST

1. **The pre-existence of Christ**
   "But as for you, Bethelehem Ephrathah, too little to be among the clans of Judah, from you One will go forth for Me to be ruler in Israel. His goings forth are from long ago, from the days of eternity" (Micah

5:2; cf. Proverbs 8:22-31; John 1:1; 1:15; 3:13; 6:51; 8:58; 17:5; Philippians 2:6; Colossians 1:17).

2. **Christ's own claims of divinity**

   a. *He claimed equality with the Father.*

   "But He answered them, 'My Father is working until now, and I Myself am working.' For this cause therefore the Jews were seeking all the more to kill Him, because He not only was breaking the Sabbath, but also was calling God His own Father, making Himself equal with God" (John 5:17-18).
   " 'I and the Father are one.' The Jews took up stones again to stone Him. Jesus answered them, 'I showed you many good works from the Father; for which of them are you stoning Me?' The Jews answered Him, 'For a good work we do not stone You, but for blasphemy; and because You, being a man, make yourself out to be God' " (John 10:30-33).

   b. *He used the divine name in reference to Himself.*

   "Jesus said to them, 'Truly, truly, I say to you, before Abraham was born, I AM' " (John 8:58; cf. Exodus 3:14; Deuteronomy 32:39; Isaiah 43:10; John 3:13; 4:26; 6:35; 8:12; 10:9; 11:25).

   c. *He is due the same honor as the Father.*

   " 'In order that all may honor the Son, even as they honor the Father. He who does not honor the Son does not honor the Father who sent Him. Truly, truly, I say to you, he who hears My word, and believes Him who sent Me, has eternal life, and does not come into judgment, but has passed out of death into life' " (John 5:23-24).

   d. *He equated knowing Him with knowing the Father.*

   "And so they were saying to Him, 'Where is Your Father?' Jesus answered, 'You know neither Me,

nor My Father; if you knew Me, you would know
My Father also ' '' (John 8:19).

e. *He said that people should believe in Him as they
believed in the Father.*

"Let not your heart be troubled; believe in God,
believe also in Me" (John 14:1; cf. 8:24).

f. *He said that in seeing Him one saw the Father.*
"Jesus said to him, 'Have I been so long with you,
and yet you have not come to know Me, Philip? He
who has seen Me has seen the Father; how do you
say, "Show us the Father"?' '' (John 14:9).

g. *He used the most intimate word to address God—
"Abba."*

"And He was saying, 'Abba! Father! All things
are possible for Thee; remove this cup from Me;
yet not what I will, but what Thou wilt.' '' (Mark
14:36; cf. Romans 8:14; Galatians 4:6). It should
be noted that no one before in the recorded history
of Israel had addressed God by such an intimate
term.

h. *The crime for which He was crucified was the
crime of blasphemy—claiming divinity or "making
Himself God."*

"But He kept silent, and made no answer. Again
the high priest was questioning Him, and saying to
Him, 'Are You the Christ, the Son of the Blessed
One?' And Jesus said, 'I am; and you shall see the
SON OF MAN SITTING AT THE RIGHT HAND OF POWER,
and COMING WITH THE CLOUDS OF HEAVEN.' And tear-
ing his clothes, the high priest said, 'What further
need do we have of witnesses? You have heard the
blasphemy; how does it seem to you?' And they
all condemned Him to be deserving of death"
(Mark 14:61-64).

3. **Divine names and titles applied to Christ.**
   a. *God*
      "Looking for the blessed hope and the appearing of the glory of our great God and Savior, Christ Jesus" (Titus 2:13; cf. John 1:1; Romans 9:5; 1 John 5:20).
   b. *Lord*
      "For this is the one referred to by Isaiah the prophet, saying, 'THE VOICE OF ONE CRYING IN THE WILDERNESS, "MAKE READY THE WAY OF THE LORD, MAKE HIS PATHS STRAIGHT!" ' " (Matthew 3:3; cf. Isaiah 40:3). "For 'WHOEVER WILL CALL UPON THE NAME OF THE LORD WILL BE SAVED' " (Romans 10:13; cf. Joel 2:32).
   c. *Son of God*
      "And Simon Peter answered and said, 'Thou art the Christ, the Son of the living God.' And Jesus answered and said to him, 'Blessed are you, Simon Barjona, because flesh and blood did not reveal this to you, but My Father who is in heaven' " (Matthew 16:16-17; cf. Luke 3:22; John 1:49; etc.).
   d. *Son of Man*
      "And as they were coming down from the mountain, Jesus commanded them, saying, 'Tell the vision to no one until the Son of Man has risen from the dead' " (Matthew 17:9; cf. 8:20; 9:6; 11:19; 12:40; 13:41; 16:13; 20:18; 24:27, 30; 25:31; Luke 18:8; 21:36; John 12:34; Acts 7:56). Please note again that this phrase "Son of Man" is not found in the New Testament on any other lips than those of Christ—except when others applied it to Him.
   e. *Jehovah God*
      Jesus claimed to be Jehovah God of the Old Testament. Below are mutual titles or acts attributed

to both Jehovah God of the Old Testament and Jesus Christ of the New Testament.*

Jesus Is Jehovah

Of Jehovah	Mutual Title or Act	Of Jesus
Isaiah 40:28	Creator	John 1:3
Isaiah 43:11; 45:22	Savior	John 4:42
1 Samuel 2:6	Raised Dead	John 5:21
Joel 3:12	Judge	John 5:27
Isaiah 60:19-20	Light	John 8:12
Exodus 3:14	I Am	John 8:58
Psalm 23:1	Shepherd	John 10:11
Isaiah 42:8; cf. 49:11	Glory of God	John 17:1,5
Isaiah 41:4; 44:6	First and Last	Revelation 1:17; 2:8
Hosea 13:14	Redeemer	Revelation 5:9
Isaiah 62:5; Hosea 2:16	Bridegroom	Matthew 25:1
Psalm 18:2	Rock	1 Corinthians 10:4
Jeremiah 31:34	Forgiver of Sins	Mark 2:7,10
Psalm 148:2	Worshiped by Angels	Hebrews 1:6
Throughout Old Testament	Addressed in Prayer	Acts 7:59
Psalm 148:5	Creator of Angels	Colossians 1:16
Isaiah 45:23	Confessed as Lord	Philippians 2:10

f. Immutability (unchangeableness)

"Jesus Christ is the same yesterday and today, yes and forever" (Hebrews 13:8; cf. 1:11-12).

g. Holiness (sinlessness)

"And we have believed and have come to know that You are the Holy One of God" (John 6:69; cf. 8:46; Matthew 27:3-4; Mark 14:55-56; Luke 23:22, 41, 47; 2 Corinthians 5:21; Hebrews 7:26; 1 Peter 1:19; 2:22; 1 John 3:5). Please remember that not only could His enemies not convict Him of sin—which they would have been delighted to do—but His closest friends affirmed His sinlessness. They were His most intimate associates.

---

*This chart, with modifications, is from Norman Geisler's *Christ: The Key to Interpreting the Bible* (Chicago: Moody, 1969), p. 48.

They had known and worked with Him for three years under every conceivable condition. This is especially significant when we realize that they were Jews, people who were religiously sensitive and from birth had been taught the sinfulness of man. Yet they uniformly attested His sinlessness.

h. *Life*

"In Him was life; and the life was the light of men" (John 1:4; cf. 14:6; 11:25).

4. **Divine works performed by and ascribed to Christ**

a. *Creation*

"For in Him all things were created, both in the heavens and on earth, visible and invisible, whether thrones or dominions or rulers or authorities—all things have been created by Him and for Him" (Colossians 1:16; cf. John 1:3, 10; 1 Corinthians 8:6; Hebrews 1:10).

b. *He upholds and preserves all things*

"And He is the radiance of His glory and the exact representation of His nature, and upholds all things by the word of His power. When He had made purification of sins, He sat down at the right hand of the Majesty on high" (Hebrews 1:3; cf. Colossians 1:17).

5. **Divine attributes ascribed to Christ**

a. *He is self-existent.*

"For just as the Father has life in Himself, even so He gave to the Son also to have life in Himself" (John 5:26; cf. 2:19: 10:17-18).

b. *He is eternal.*

"But of the Son He says, 'THY THRONE, O GOD, IS FOREVER AND EVER, AND THE RIGHTEOUS SCEPTER IS THE SCEPTER OF HIS KINGDOM' " (Hebrews 1:8). "And, 'THOU, LORD, IN THE BEGINNING DIDST LAY THE FOUNDATION OF THE EARTH, AND THE HEAVENS ARE THE WORKS OF THY HANDS; THEY WILL PERISH, BUT THOU RE-

MAINEST; AND THEY ALL WILL BECOME OLD AS A GAR-
MENT, AND AS A MANTLE THOU WILT ROLL THEM UP; AS A
GARMENT THEY WILL ALSO BE CHANGED. BUT THOU ART
THE SAME, AND THY YEARS WILL NOT COME TO AN
END' '' (Hebrews 1:10-12; cf. John 1:1-2; 17:5, 24; I
John 1:2).

c. *He is omnipresent (present in all places at all times).*

"Teaching them to observe all that I commanded
you; and lo, I am with you always, even to the end
of the age" (Matthew 28:20; cf. 18:20; John 3:13;
Ephesians 1:21).

d. *He is omniscient (having all knowledge).*

"But Jesus, on His part, was not entrusting Himself to them, for He knew all men, and because He
did not need anyone to bear witness concerning
man for He Himself knew what was in man"
(John 2:24-25; cf. Matthew 9:4; 12:25; Mark 2:8;
Luke 6:8; 9:47; 10:22; John 1:48; 10:15; 16:30;
21:17; Colossians 2:3; Revelation 2:23).

e. *He is omnipotent (having all power and authority).*

"And Jesus came up and spoke to them, saying,
'All authority has been given to Me in heaven and
on earth' '' (Matthew 28:18; cf. Luke 21:15; John
1:3; 10:18; 1 Corinthians 1:24; Ephesians 1:22;
Philippians 3:21; Colossians 2:10; Revelation
1:18).

f. *He forgives sins.*

"And seeing their faith, He said, 'Friend, your
sins are forgiven you.' And the scribes and the
Pharisees began to reason, saying, 'Who is this
man who speaks blasphemies? Who can forgive
sins, but God alone?' But Jesus, aware of their
reasonings, answered and said to them, 'Why are
you reasoning in your hearts? Which is easier, to

say, "Your sins have been forgiven you," or to say, "Rise and walk"? But in order that you may know that the Son of Man has authority on earth to forgive sins,' He said to the paralytic, 'I say to you, rise, and take up your stretcher and go home' " (Luke 5:20-24; cf. Matthew 9:5-6; Mark 2:5-11; Luke 7:47-49; Acts 5:31).

g. *He gives the Holy Spirit.*

"But I tell you the truth, it is to your advantage that I go away; for if I do not go away, the Helper shall not come to you; but if I go, I will send Him to you" (John 16:7; cf. 20:22; Acts 2:33).

h. *He gives peace.*

"Peace I leave with you; My peace I give to you; not as the world gives, do I give to you. Let not your heart be troubled, nor let it be fearful" (John 14:27; cf. 16:33; Romans 15:33; 16:20; 2 Corinthians 13:11; Philippians 4:9; 1 Thessalonians 5:23; Hebrews 13:20).

i. *He gives light.*

"Again therefore Jesus spoke to them, saying, 'I am the light of the world; he who follows Me shall not walk in the darkness, but shall have the light of life" (John 8:12; cf. 1:4-9; 9:5; 12:35, 46; 1 John 1:5-7; Revelation 21:23).

j. *He gives eternal life.*

"Even as Thou gavest Him authority over all mankind, that to all whom Thou hast given Him, He may give eternal life" (John 17:2).

k. *He confers spiritual gifts.*

"Therefore it says, 'When He ascended on high, He led captive a host of captives, and He gave gifts to men.' (Now this expression, 'He ascended,' what does it mean except that He also had descended into the lower parts of the earth? He who descended is Himself also He who ascended far above all the heavens, that He might fill all things.) And He gave some as apostles, and some as prophets, and some as evangelists, and some as pastors and teachers, for the equipping of the saints for the work of service, to the building up of the body of Christ; until we all attain to the unity of the faith, and of the knowledge of the Son of God, to a mature man, to the measure of the stature which belongs to the fulness of Christ'' (Ephesians 4:8-13).

l. He exercised power over the natural order.
  (1) He calmed storms (Mark 4:35-41).
  (2) He walked on water (Matthew 14:22-27).

m. He cured mental disorders.
  ''And just then there was in their synagogue a man with an unclean spirit; and he cried out, saying, 'What do we have to do with You, Jesus of Nazareth? Have You come to destroy us? I know who You are—the Holy One of God!' And Jesus rebuked him, saying, 'Be quiet, and come out of him!' And throwing him into convulsions, the unclean spirit cried out with a loud voice, and came out of him'' (Mark 1:23-26; cf. 5:1-20; Matthew 8:28-34; Mark 3:11-12; Luke 8:26-39).

n. He healed the incurably sick.
  ''And He answered and said to them, 'Go and report to John what you have seen and heard: the BLIND RECEIVE SIGHT, the lame walk, the lepers are cleansed, and the deaf hear, the dead are raised up, the POOR HAVE THE GOSPEL PREACHED TO THEM.' '' (Luke 7:22; cf. Matthew 8:1-4; Mark 2:10-11; 3:1-6; 13:10-13; John 5:2-9; 9:1-11).

o. He raised people from the dead.
  And it came about soon afterwards, that He went to a city called Nain; and His disciples were going along with Him, accompanied by a large mul-

titude. Now as He approached the gate of the city, behold, a dead man was being carried out, the only son of his mother, and she was a widow; and a sizeable crowd from the city was with her. And when the Lord saw her, He felt compassion for her, and said to her, "Do not weep." And He came up and touched the coffin; and the bearers came to a halt. And He said, "Young man, I say to you, arise!" And the dead man sat up, and began to speak. And Jesus gave him back to his mother. And fear gripped them all, and they began glorifying God, saying, "A great prophet has arisen among us!" and, "God has visited His people!" And this report concerning Him went out all over Judea, and in all the surrounding district. (Luke 7:11-17; cf. 8:49-56; John 11:17-44).

p. *He will raise all men from the dead.*

"And He gave Him authority to execute judgment, because He is the Son of Man. Do not marvel at this; for an hour is coming, in which all who are in the tombs shall hear His voice, and shall come forth; those who did the good deeds, to a resurrection of life, those who committed the evil deeds to a resurrection of judgment' " (John 5:27-29).

q. *He will judge all men.*

"For we must all appear before the judgment seat of Christ, that each one may be recompensed for his deeds in the body, according to what he has done, whether good or bad" (2 Corinthians 5:10; cf. Matthew 25:31-46; Revelation 20:11-15).

6. **Divine Worship Is Offered to Christ.**

"And when they got into the boat, the wind stopped. And those who were in the boat worshiped Him, saying, 'You are certainly God's Son!' " (Matthew 14:32-33; cf. 8:2; John 9:29-38; 20:27-29; Hebrews

1:6; Revelation 5:13-14.) Acts 10:25-26 and Revelation 19:10 show that to fall down in homage is the greatest act of worship and adoration, and is appropriate only to God.

7. **Prayer is offered in His name and directed to Him.**
   " 'You did not choose Me, but I chose you, and appointed you, that you should go and bear fruit, and that your fruit should remain, that whatever you ask of the Father in My name, He may give to you' " (John 15:16; cf. 14:13-14; 15:7; Acts 1:24; 7:59-60). Also, note here the doxologies, ascriptions of praise, and benedictions to Christ (Romans 1:7; 2 Corinthians 13:14; 2 Peter 3:18; Revelation 1:5-6).

8. **Others attributed divinity to Him.**
   "Thomas answered and said to Him, 'My Lord and my God!' " (John 20:28; cf. Matthew 16:15-17; Luke 3:22; Acts 2:36; 7:59; Philippians 2:9-11; Colossians 2:9; Hebrews 1:3, 8: Titus 2:13: 2 Peter 1:1).

I have found three basic statements concerning the nature of the incarnate Christ very helpful. They encompass the true nature of Christ's incarnation:

- *Christ was undiminished deity.* By that we mean that Jesus was no less God when He was man than when He was God before He became man. There was no change at all in His essence as God. In becoming man Christ did not empty Himself of any attribute relevant to His essence as God. If He had done so then He was not God, and if He is not God, then there is no Savior! God in His essence is immutable, or unchanging. So in becoming Man He gave up the *existence* of God (heaven) but not the *essence* of God. In His incarnation, He brought the essence of God into the existence of man. Jesus Christ then has always been perfect God—even when He became a perfect man; and while He was a perfect man, He never ceased to be perfect God. So first, Jesus Christ was undiminished deity.

- But *He was also true and complete humanity.* He was everything that was essential to manhood. He grew, He hungered, He thirsted, He was tired, and so on. The only thing that was different about His humanity was that it was sinless. But sin is not essential to humanity—it is rather a parasitic invasion. So Jesus was neither God acting as a man, nor a good man who somehow achieved divinity. His true nature is undiminished deity and complete humanity.

- Third, *these two natures of Christ—divine and human—are united in one person forever.* We cannot therefore either confuse the natures or divide the person. His divine nature was never absorbed into the human, or His human nature absorbed into the divine. He is not two persons, but one person with two natures. He is fully God and fully man.

Those three statements may sound technical and theological, but they are in fact intensely practical. They are in complete accord with biblical revelation and will help one better understand and explain the pre-existence and incarnation of Christ.

Conclusions

A basic law of logic says that *things equal to the same thing are equal to each other.* It is clear from the above points that the attributes and ascriptions of God found in the Bible are equally ascribed to Christ—and, as we shall see, to the Holy Spirit. Christ also both made the claims of God and accepted the prerogatives of God. All these claims, attributes, prerogatives, and ascriptions of divinity clearly point out that not only did Christ claim divinity, but it is ascribed to Him throughout the entire New Testament. Such an attitude of mind in others on His behalf would be idolatry, and His acceptance of their worship would be megalomania, if He were indeed not God incarnate. So the aforementioned Scriptures are conclusive proof for the divinity of Christ. They destroy Mr. Wierwille's arguments completely and sever the vital doctrinal nerve of The Way movement.

Appendix 2:

Apologetic for the Triunity of God

Although no single passage in Scripture sets forth the doctrine of the Trinity in formal, creedal statement, there are numerous passages in which the three Persons are mentioned in such a manner as to exhibit at once Their *unity* and Their *distinctness*. Many passages could be cited to verify this. I shall, however, list only several Old and New Testament verses to point out that the triunity of God is set forth from Genesis to Revelation.

Old Testament:
1. "Let *Us* make man in Our image" (Genesis 1:26, emphasis added).
2. "Come, let *Us* go down and there confuse their language" (Genesis 11:7, emphasis added).
3. "Whom shall I send, and who will go for *Us*?" (Isaiah 6:8, emphasis added).

New Testament:
1. *Birth of Jesus* (Matthew 1:18-23; Luke 1:35)
   These passages record the announcement about the birth's being of God, that the Holy Spirit would make it possible, and that Christ would be conceived and

born. Clearly the ministry of the triune Godhead of Father, Son, and Holy Spirit.

2. *Christ's baptism* (Matthew 3:16-17)

   In this passage we find the Son, or second member of the Godhead, being baptized, the voice from God the Father, and the testimony of the Spirit as a descending dove. Again, Father, Son, and Holy Spirit.

3. *Great commission* (Matthew 28:19)

   Jesus commissioned His disciples here to baptize believers in the name of the Father, Son, and Holy Spirit. Therefore, the trinitarian baptismal formula is practiced by all branches of orthodox Christianity to this day.

4. *Paraclete passage* (John 14:16, 17, 26; 15:26; 16:7-14)

5. *High priestly prayer* (John 17:1-26)

   Here the Son prayed to the Father in behalf of His disciples. The Son's speaking of the glory He had shared with the Father "before the world was," (17:5) and of the love the Father had for the Son "before the foundation of the world" (17:24) is another clear testimony to the pre-existence of Christ in the Godhead.

6. *Sin of Ananias and Sapphira* (Acts 5:3-5)

   Here we see the Holy Spirit clearly called God. Peter asks, "Why has Satan filled your heart to lie to the Holy Spirit?" (v.3). He then says, "You have not lied to men, but to God" (v. 4). Here the Holy Spirit is proved to be both a person—you cannot lie to an "it" or a nonentity—and God.

7. *The commissioning of Barnabas and Paul* (Acts 13:2-4)

   Again the Holy Spirit is revealed as a person: "The Holy Spirit said, 'Set apart for Me Barnabas and Saul for the work to which I have called them' " (v. 2). The Holy Spirit calls and commissions, functions that are prerogatives only of God and possibilities only of a person and not an "it" of a divine influence.

8. *The gifts of the Holy Spirit* (1 Corinthians 12:7)
"The same Spirit works all these things, distributing to each one individually just as He wills" (v. 11). Again is seen the sovereign work of a divine being who has a will—something only a person can have. Paul begins this passage with a Trinitarian statement: "the same Spirit. . . . the same Lord. . . . the same God" (v. 4-6).

9. *Apostolic benediction* (2 Corinthians 13:14)
"Jesus Christ [God the Son], and the love of God [the Father], and the fellowship of the Holy Spirit [God the Spirit], be with you all."

From Genesis to Revelation, the Bible establishes the *unity* of God (Exodus 20:3; Deuteronomy 6:4; Isaiah 44:6; John 10:30; 1 Corinthians 8:4; Ephesians 4:5-6; James 2:19; Revelation 22:13). But although God in His innermost nature is One, He nevertheless exists in three Persons, referred to in Scriptures as "Father," "Son," and "Holy Spirit." These Three are one God, the same in *substance* and *equal* in power and glory. The following verses show conclusively that divinity is *equally ascribed* to the Three Persons within the Godhead.

- *The Father is God.* "Yet for us there is but one God, the Father, from whom are all things, and we exist for Him; and one Lord, Jesus Christ, through whom are all things, and we exist through Him" (1 Corinthians 8:6; cf. Matthew 11:25; Mark 14:36; John 4:23-24; 6:27; 11:41; 17:11; 20:17; Galatians 1:1; Ephesians 4:6; Philippians 2:11; 1 Peter 1:2).
- *The Son is God.* "Looking for the blessed hope and the appearing of the glory of our great God and Savior, Christ Jesus" (Titus 2:13; cf. Matthew 16:16; Mark 2:5-10; John 1:1; 5:18; 10:30; 20:28; Romans 9:5; Colossians 2:9).

- *The Spirit is God.* "But Peter said, 'Ananias, why has Satan filled your heart to lie to the Holy Spirit, and to keep back some of the price of the land? While it remained unsold, did it not remain your own? And after it was sold, was it not under your control? Why is it that you have conceived this deed in your heart? You have not lied to men, but to God.' And as he heard these words, Ananias fell down and breathed his last; and great fear came upon all who heard of it" (Acts 5:3-5; cf. Matthew 28:19; John 15:26; 1 Corinthians 2:11; 2 Corinthians 13:14).

We can clearly see that the Holy Spirit is placed on a plane of absolute equality with the Father and the Son as deity and is equally regarded with them as the source of all power and blessing.

DIVINE ATTRIBUTES OF THE HOLY SPIRIT

1. **Eternity**
   "How much more will the blood of Christ, who through the *eternal Spirit* offered Himself without blemish to God, cleanse your conscience from dead works to serve the living God?" (Hebrews 9:14, emphasis added).

2. **Omnipresence**
   "Where can I go from Thy Spirit? Or where can I flee from Thy presence? If I ascend to heaven, Thou art there; if I make my bed in Sheol, behold, Thou art there. If I take the wings of the dawn, if I dwell in the remotest part of the sea, even there Thy hand will lead me, and Thy right hand will lay hold of me. If I say, 'Surely the darkness will overwhelm me, and the light around me will be night,' even the darkness is not dark to Thee, and the night is as bright as the day. Darkness and light are alike to Thee" (Psalm 139:7-12).

3. **Omniscience**
   a. *He has wisdom and understanding.* "And the Spirit of the LORD will rest on Him, the spirit of wisdom and understanding, the spirit of counsel and strength, the spirit of knowledge and the fear of the LORD" (Isaiah 11:2).
   b. *He has perfect knowledge.* "For the Spirit searches all things, even the depths of God. . . . No one knows the thoughts of God except the Spirit of God" (1 Corinthians 2:10-11).
   c. *He has a mind.* "And He who searches the hearts knows what the mind of the Spirit is, because He intercedes for the saints according to the will of God" (Romans 8:27).

4. **He has will**
   "But one and the same Spirit works all these things, distributing to each one individually just as He wills" (1 Corinthians 12:11).

5. **He has emotions**
   The Holy Spirit may be:
   a. *Grieved.* "And do not grieve the Holy Spirit of God, by whom you were sealed for the day of redemption" (Ephesians 4:30; cf. Isaiah 63:10).
   b. *He may be resisted.* "You men who are stiff-necked and uncircumcised in heart and ears are always resisting the Holy Spirit; you are doing just as your fathers did" (Acts 7:51).

CONCLUSION

Throughout the Scriptures, then, the Holy Spirit is set forth as a *distinct person,* having mind, will, emotions, and power of His own (Matthew 12:31-32; Luke 12:12; John 14:16-17; 15:26; 16:13-14; Romans 8:26; Ephesians 4:30; Revelation 2:17). In the Bible, personal pronouns "He," "Him," "I," and "Me" are applied to

Him—pronouns that can be used intelligently only when applied to a person. They occur so repeatedly in the Scriptures that they connot be set aside as a tendency to personify an impersonal force. This conclusively proves to anyone who accepts the Scriptures as authoritative that the Holy Spirit *is not* a "synonym for God" or "a spiritual ability," as Mr. Wierwille says, but *the third Person of the triune God.*

We are faced then with these alternatives: Either the Christian doctrine of the Trinity must be true, or the Scriptures are contradictory. Either the Scriptures recognize more gods than one, or Christ together with the Father and the Holy Spirit is that one God.

Cult Resource Groups

1. Spiritual Counterfeits Project
   P.O. Box 4309
   Berkeley, CA 94704

2. Eastern Mysticism Project
   (Project Director: Pat Means)
   The Mystical Maze (book)
   The Mystics (film)
   Order from:
   Campus Crusade for Christ
   Arrowhead Springs
   San Bernardino, CA 92414

3. Christ for the Cults
   (Director: Erich Grieshaber)
   P.O. Box 4295
   Santa Clara, CA 95050

4. The Christian Research Institute
   Dr. Walter Martin
   P.O. Box 500
   San Juan Capistrano, CA 92675

5. CARIS
   (Christian Apologetics:
   Research and Information Service)
   P.O. Box 1783
   Santa Ana, CA 92702

   Literature Department:
   P.O. Box 265
   Whittier, CA 90608

6. COUP
   (Cultic and Occultic Unification Program)
   P.O. Box 80
   Scotsdale, AZ 85252

7. Conservative Baptist Theological Seminary
   10,000 University Park Station
   Denver, CO 80201

   (Ask for outlines by Dr. Gordon R. Lewis. He has
   made available pamphlets on Hare Krishna, Zen
   Buddhism, the Divine Light Mission, and other
   Eastern religions.)

8. Institute of Contemporary Christianity
   (James Bjornstad, Executive Director)
   Box A
   Oakland, NJ 07436

9. C.H.A.O.S. Ltd.
   Research and Information Service on
   Cults, Heresies, and Occult Sects
   P.O. Box 6224
   Oakland, CA 94603

10. Jesus People, U.S.A.
    4431 N. Paulina
    Chicago, IL 60640

11. Watchman Fellowship
    "An Evangelical Lay Ministry to the Cults"
    P.O. Box 7681
    Columbus, GA 31908

12. COPAC
    Citizens Organized for Public Awareness
       of Cults
    P.O. Box 3194
    Greensboro, NC 27402

13. The New Directions Evangelistic Association
    P.O. Box 2347
    Burlington, NC 27215

Suggested Reading List

Bjornstad, James. *The Moon Is Not the Son*. Minneapolis: Bethany Fellowship, 1976.

Boa, Kenneth. *Cults, World Religions, and You*. Wheaton, Ill.: Victor, 1977.

Enroth, Ronald. *Youth Brainwashing and the Extremist Cults*. Grand Rapids: Zondervan, 1977.

The God-men Witness Lee and the Local Church. Berkeley, Calif: Spiritual Counterfeits Project, 1977.

Hefley, James. *The Youth Nappers*. Wheaton, Ill.: Victor, 1977.

Levitt, Zola. *The Spirit of Sun Myung Moon*. Irvine, Calif.: Harvest, 1976.

Lewis, Gordon. *What Everyone Should Know About Transcendental Meditation*. Glendale, Calif.: Regal, 1976.

Lifton, Robert. *Thought Reform and the Psychology of Totalism*. New York: Norton, 1963.

McBeth, Leon. *Strange New Religions*. Nashville: Broadman, 1977.

Martin, Walter. *The Kingdom of the Cults*. Minneapolis: Bethany Fellowship, 1968.

Means, Pat. *The Mystical Maze*. San Bernardino, Calif.: Campus Crusade, 1976.

Patrick, Ted. *Let Our Children Go*. New York: Dutton, 1976.

Peterson, William J.. *Those Curious New Cults*. New Canaan, Conn.: Keats, 1975.

Sparks, Jack. *The Mind Benders*. New York: Nelson, 1977.

Stott, John. *Your Mind Matters*. Downers Grove, Ill.: InterVarsity, 1972.

Verdier, Paul A. *Brainwashing and the Cults: An Expose on Capturing the Human Mind*. North Hollywood, Calif.: Wilshire, 1977.

Yamamoto, J. Isamu. *The Puppet Master*. Downers Grove, Ill.: InterVarsity, 1977.

Notes

2

1. Elena S. Whiteside, *The Way: Living in Love,* 2d ed. (New Knoxville, Ohio: American Christian, 1974), p. 172.
2. Ibid., pp. 172-73.
3. Vince McKelvey, "Charisma: Way Founder Wierwille Seen as Either Loving, Warm or 'Own Worst Enemy,' " Dayton (Ohio) *Journal Herald,* April 3, 1979.
4. Whiteside, pp. 174-175.
5. Ibid., p. 186.
6. Victor Paul Wierwille, *Power for Abundant Living* (New Knoxville, Ohio: American Christian, 1971), p. 3.
7. Whiteside, p. 177.
8. Ibid., p. 187.
9. Ibid.
10. Ibid., p. 178.
11. Ibid., pp. 180-81.
12. Transcript of a recorded interview of Victor Paul Wierwille by Art Toalston, correspondent for the *National Courier,* in Mr. Wierwille's office at The Way headquarters, New Knoxville, Ohio, February 1976, p. 11.
13. Ibid.
14. Whiteside, p. 187.
15. Vince McKelvey, "Growth: The Way Tree Has Branched Out, but Expansion Brings Criticism," Dayton (Ohio) *Journal Herald,* April 2, 1979.
16. Whiteside, p. 203.
17. Ibid., p. 190.
18. McKelvey, "Charisma."

19. McKelvey, "Growth."
20. Whiteside, p. 91.
21. Victor Paul Wierwille, *Jesus Christ Is Not God* (New Knoxville, Ohio: American Christian, 1975), p. 180.
22. Herbert Diamond, "A Degree from Pike's Peak," *Christianity Today,* November 21, 1975, pp. 19-20.
23. McKelvey, "Charisma."
24. Whiteside, p. 189.
25. Transcript of Toalston's interview, p. 40.
26. Whiteside, p. 43.
27. Ibid., p. 252.
28. Transcript of a talk by Victor Paul Wierwille at a Way rally recorded by J. L. Williams in Raleigh, North Carolina, fall 1975.
29. Victor Paul Wierwille, *How to Speak in Tongues* (New Knoxville, Ohio: American Christian, n.d.), p. 102.

3

1. Elena S. Whiteside, *The Way: Living in Love,* 2d ed. (New Knoxville, Ohio: American Christian, 1974), p. 30.
2. Ibid., p. 184.
3. Transcript of a recorded interview of Victor Paul Wierwille by Art Toalston in Mr. Wierwille's office at The Way headquarters, New Knoxville, Ohio, February 1976, p. 5.
4. PFAL brochure; this brochure was also an insert in *The Way Magazine,* September/October 1977.
5. Whiteside, p. 29.
6. Transcript of a talk by Victor Paul Wierwille at a Way rally recorded by J. L. Williams in Raleigh, North Carolina, fall 1975.
7. Jack Sparks, "The Way International," in *The Mindbenders* (New York: Nelson, 1977), pp. 188-89.
8. Kevin N. Springer, "Victor Paul Wierwille and The Way" paper published May 20, 1975, at Grace Haven Farms, Mansfield, Ohio.

9. Ibid.
10. *This Is the Way,* promotional brochure of The Way International.
11. Ibid.
12. "Preaching Deliverance to the Captives," *The Way Magazine,* March/April 1978, p. 25.
13. *This Is The Way.*
14. Vince McKelvey, "Way's Assets Draw Criticism," Dayton (Ohio) *Journal Herald,* April 4, 1979.

4

1. Victor Paul Wierwille, *Jesus Christ Is Not God* (New Knoxville, Ohio: American Christian, 1975), p. 4.
2. Victor Paul Wierwille, *Power for Abundant Living* (New Knoxville, Ohio: American Christian, 1971), pp. 272-73.

5

1. Transcript of a recorded interview of Victor Paul Wierwille by Art Toalston in Mr. Wierwille's office at The Way headquarters, New Knoxville, Ohio, February 1976, p. 32.
2. Ibid., p. 19.
3. Cathy Port, "Our Times," *The Way Magazine,* January/February 1978, p. 22.
4. Hal Miller, "The Way Followers March on New Knoxville Church," St. Mary's (Ohio) *Evening Leader,* October 17, 1977.
5. Victor Paul Wierwille, *Jesus Christ Is Not God* (New Knoxville, Ohio: American Christian, 1975), p. 5.
6. Ibid., p. 8.
7. Ibid., p. 79.

8. Ibid., p. 71.
9. Ibid., pp. 6-7.
10. Transcript of J. L. William's recording of a Way rally, Raleigh, North Carolina, fall 1975.
11. M. R. Vincent, *Word Studies in the New Testament,* 4 vols. (Grand Rapids: Eerdmans, 1957), 2:53-54.
12. Elena S. Whiteside, *The Way: Living in Love,* 2d ed. (New Knoxville, Ohio: American Christian, 1974), p. 209.
13. Earle E. Cairns, *Christianity Through the Centuries* (Grand Rapids: Zondervan, 1973), pp. 111-12.
14. Wierwille, *Jesus Christ Is Not God,* p. 79.
15. Ibid., pp. 28-29, 85.
16. Ibid., p. 81.
17. Ibid., p. 85.
18. Ibid., p. 83.
19. Ibid., p. 91.
20. Ibid., p. 98.
21. Ibid., p. 102.

6

1. *The Way Magazine,* January/February 1978, p. 6.
2. Transcript of a recorded interview of Victor Paul Wierwille by Art Toalston in Mr. Wierwille's office at The Way headquarters, New Knoxville, Ohio, February, 1976, p. 2.
3. Ibid., p. 8.
4. Ibid., p. 15.
5. Ibid.
6. R. C. Anderson, North Carolina Way director, to J. L. Williams, July 6, 1978.
7. Transcript of Toalston's interview, pp. 9, 29.
8. Victor Paul Wierwille, *Jesus Christ Is Not God* (New Knoxville, Ohio, 1975), p. 19.
9. Ibid., p. 31.
10. Ibid., p. 100.
11. Ibid., p. 115.

12. Transcript of Toalston's interview, p. 14.
13. C. S. Lewis, *Mere Christianity* (New York: Macmillan, 1943, 1945, 1952), p. 120.
14. Transcript of Toalston's interview, p. 5.

7

1. Hal Miller, "The Way Followers March on New Knoxville Church," St. Mary's (Ohio) *Evening Leader,* October 17, 1977.
2. Transcript of a recorded interview of Victor Paul Wierwille by Art Toalston in Mr. Wierwille's office at The Way headquarters, New Knoxville, Ohio, February 1976, p. 6.
3. Victor Paul Wierwille, *Jesus Christ Is Not God* (New Knoxville, Ohio: American Christian, 1975), p. 2.
4. Transcript of Toalston's interview, p. 34.
5. Wierwille, *Jesus Christ Is Not God,* p. 3.
6. Transcript of Toalston's interview, p. 15.
7. Wierwille, *Jesus Christ Is Not God,* pp. 7, 25.
8. Ibid., p. 26.
9. Jack Sparks, "The Way International," in *The Mindbenders* (New York: Nelson, 1977), p. 191.
10. Wierwille, *Jesus Christ Is Not God,* p. 23.
11. G. L. Carey, "Council of Nicea," in the *New International Dictionary of the Christian Church,* edited by J. D. Douglas (Grand Rapids: Zondervan, 1974), p. 706.
12. F. F. Bruce, *The Spreading Flame* (Grand Rapids: Eerdmans, 1958), p. 304.
13. Wierwille, *Jesus Christ Is Not God,* p. 24.
14. Bruce, p. 306.
15. Sparks, p. 192.
16. Ibid.

17. C. S. Lewis, *Mere Christianity* (New York: Macmillan, 1943, 1945, 1952), p. 126.
18. Ibid., pp. 33, 126-27.
19. Wierwille, *Jesus Christ Is Not God,* pp. 11-12.
20. Lewis, *Mere Christianity,* p. 29.
21. C. S. Lewis, "Answers to Questions on Christianity," in *God in the Dock* (Grand Rapids: Eerdmans, 1970), p. 54.
22. Ibid., "Christian Apologetics," in *God in the Dock,* p. 102.

8

1. Elena S. Whiteside, *The Way: Living in Love,* 2d ed. (New Knoxville, Ohio: American Christian, 1974), p. 209.
2. Victor Paul Wierwille, *Jesus Christ Is Not God* (New Knoxville, Ohio: American Christian, 1975), p. 127.
3. Victor Paul Wierwille, *Receiving the Holy Spirit Today* (New Knoxville, Ohio: American Christian, 1972), pp. 4-5.
4. Victor Paul Wierwille, *Power for Abundant Living* (New Knoxville, Ohio: American Christian, 1971), p. 258.
5. Whiteside, p. 201.
6. Ibid., p. 196.
7. Ibid., pp. 197-200.
8. Transcript of a recorded interview of Victor Paul Wierwille by Art Toalston in Mr. Wierwille's office at The Way headquarters, New Knoxville, Ohio, February 1976, p. 33.
9. Wierwille, *Jesus Christ Is Not God,* p. 131.
10. Victor Paul Wierwille, "What Is True Worship?" *The Way Magazine,* May/June 1978, p. 6.
11. Transcript of Toalston's interview, p. 35.
12. Victor Paul Wierwille, *How to Speak in Tongues* (New Knoxville, Ohio: American Christian, n.d.), pp. 8-9.

9

1. Transcript of a recorded interview of Victor Paul Wierwille by Art Toalston in Mr. Wierwille's office at The Way headquarters, New Knoxville, Ohio, February 1976, p. 39.
2. Transcript of a talk by Victor Paul Wierwille at a Way rally recorded by J. L. Williams in Raleigh, North Carolina, fall 1975.
3. Elena S. Whiteside, *The Way: Living in Love,* 2d ed. (New Knoxville, Ohio: American Christian, 1972), p. 178.
4. Transcript of William's recording of Wierwille's talk at Way rally.
5. Ibid.
6. Ibid.
7. Transcript of Toalston's interview, p. 29.
8. Walter J. Cummins, "In Search of the God-breathed Originals," *The Way Magazine,* March/April 1976, p. 10.
9. Transcript of Toalston's interview, p. 20.
10. Ibid.
11. Cummins, p. 10-11.
12. Ibid.
13. Richard N. Longenecker and Merrill C. Tenney, eds., *New Dimensions in Evangelical New Testament Studies* (Grand Rapids: Zondervan, 1974), pp. 134, 143.
14. Norman L. Geisler and William E. Nix, *A General Introduction to the Bible* (Chicago: Moody, 1968), p. 217.
15. Ibid., p. 219.
16. Ibid., p. 218.

10

1. Victor Paul Wierwille, *The Word's Way* (New Knoxville, Ohio: American Christian, 1971), pp. 267-73.
2. Victor Paul Wierwille, *Are the Dead Alive Now?* (New

Knoxville, Ohio: American Christian, 1973), pp. 21-49.

3. Victor Paul Wierwille, *Jesus Christ Is Not God* (New Knoxville, Ohio, 1975), p. 19.

11

1. Victor Paul Wierwille, *The New, Dynamic Church* (New Knoxville, Ohio: American Christian, 1971), p. 108.

2. Victor Paul Wierwille, *The Bible Tells Me So* (New Knoxville, Ohio: American Christian, 1971), p. 5.

3. Victor Paul Wierwille, *The Word's Way* (New Knoxville, Ohio: American Chrisitan, 1971), p. 266.

4. Victor Paul Wierwille, *Jesus Christ Is Not God* (New Knoxville, Ohio: American Christian, 1975), p. 3.

13

1. Reprinted, with changes, from J. L. Williams, *Identifying and Dealing with the Cults* (Burlington, N.C.: New Directions, 1974), pp. 21-34 and appendix 3, pp. 1-3.

BIBLIOGRAPHY

Books:

Bruce, F. F. *The Spreading Flame.* Grand Rapids: Eerdmans, 1958.

Cairns, Earle E. *Christianity Through the Centuries.* Grand Rapids: Zondervan, 1973.

Geisler, Norman L., and Nix, William E. *A General Introduction to the Bible.* Chicago: Moody, 1968.

Lewis, C. S. *God in the Dock.* Grand Rapids: Eerdmans, 1970.

————. *Mere Christianity.* New York: Macmillan, 1943, 1945, 1952.

Longnecker, Richard N., and Tenney, Merrill C.; eds. *New Dimensions in New Testament Study.* Grand Rapids: Zondervan, 1974.

Sparks, Jack. *The Mindbenders.* New York: Nelson, 1977.

Vincent, M. R. *Word Studies in the New Testament.* 4 vols. Grand Rapids: Eerdmans, 1957.

Whiteside, Elena S. *The Way: Living in Love.* 2nd ed. New Knoxville, Ohio: American Christian, 1974.

Wierwille, Victor Paul. *Are the Dead Alive Now?* New Knoxville, Ohio: American Christian, 1973.

————. *The Bible Tells Me So.* New Knoxville, Ohio: American Christian, 1971.

————. *How to Speak in Tongues.* New Knoxville, Ohio: American Christian, n.d.

————. *Jesus Christ Is Not God*. New Knoxville, Ohio: American Christian, 1975.

————. *The New, Dynamic Church*. New Knoxville, Ohio: American Christian, 1971.

————. *Power for Abundant Living*. New Knoxville, Ohio: American Christian, 1971.

————. *Receiving the Holy Spirit Today*. New Knoxville, Ohio: American Christian, 1972.

————. *The Word's Way*. New Knoxville, Ohio: American Christian, 1971.

Periodicals:

McKelvey, Vince. Series of articles concerning The Way and Victor Paul Wierwille. *Journal Herald* (Dayton, Ohio), 2, 3, 4 April 1979.

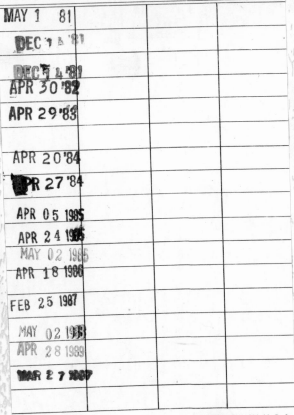

DATE DUE

MAY 1 81		
DEC 1 A '81		
DEC 1 4 '81		
APR 30 '82		
APR 29 '83		
APR 20 '84		
APR 27 '84		
APR 05 1985		
APR 24 1985		
MAY 02 1985		
APR 18 1900		
FEB 25 1987		
MAY 02 198		
APR 28 1989		
MAR 2 7 1987		